Motherless

A Novel by
Kinyatta E. Gray

Motherless© by Kinyatta E. Gray, Copyright 2021

Publishing Services By: Pen Legacy, LLC
Cover By: Christian Cuan
Edited By: Robyn Latice

Library of Congress Cataloging – in- Publication Data has been applied for.

ISBN: 978-1-7373494-0-2

First Edition
PRINTED IN THE UNITED STATES OF AMERICA.

HONORING

Ms. Bee

This book is dedicated to the "Motherless".

The accomplishment of writing and releasing
this book is dedicated to the memory of
Beverly E. Carroll (1958-2018).

"They can't rescue you, if they don't know that you need help. Ask for help to fight another day."

~UNKNOWN

Motherless

Prologue

Betrayal Knows No Family

Screams tore through the air but barely came from the badly wounded woman lying on the cold theater room floor. Instead, she coughed and wheezed, spitting out blood intermittently, while the tearful younger lady applying pressure to her wounds could barely contain herself.

On what was meant to be a lovely Friday night, Bella Chloe Monroe never would have imagined her hands would be plugging wounds on her mother's body instead of yanking lobsters from their shells at their dinner reservation. It wasn't a reality she could have drawn up, and she was certain it wasn't one her mother could have foreseen either.

"Pick me up at the theatre by eight," were the words the grey-haired lady had said to her child on the phone. *"I love you and hope to see you soon,"* had followed shortly.

Bella rang those words in her head while she dialed her mom's phone as she stood outside the theater to pick her up. Her cellphone barely connected, and regardless of how many times she called out to the woman, she just wouldn't respond.

"Oh my God!"

Bella gasped at the sight of blood squirting from her mother's neck. She yanked her right hand from the gaping wound on her mother's chest, right above the heart, and placed it over the lengthy one on the side of her neck. Her left hand simultaneously moved away from a bleeding spot on the old woman's abdomen and covered where her right hand had previously been.

"Stay with me, Mama! Stay with me!" Bella cried out in a fearful tone.

Her purse, holding her cellphone, was just a few feet away yet felt like miles from where she knelt. Unsure of what could become of her mother if she took those few seconds to reach the phone and place a call for an ambulance, she continued to press down on the wounds and cry atop her voice in hopes someone would hear her.

"Help! Somebody help!" she screamed to no avail.

It was nighttime, and nobody was meant to be at the

theatre house. With ample renovations ongoing for the big event scheduled to happen in a week, everyone had been given days off so the construction crew could put their finishing touch on things. In hindsight, Bella felt stupid for suggesting it to her mother. She couldn't help but feel herself slowly begin to tear with guilt on the inside.

Torn between applying pressure on her mother's wound and getting her cellphone, she opted for the latter, hoping and praying it just might save the woman. The past five minutes had trickled past like it was an hour, and she could have sworn she had been there the entire day had it not been for her watch beeping aloud to indicate it was five minutes past eight—the exact time of their reservation at Chandler's Restaurant.

"Hang in there!" she called out to her mother, who had gone limp and was barely moving her arms. "Please don't move. Please don't attempt to move."

Through her glassy vision, Bella managed to punch the numbers 9-1-1 into her cellphone while she hurried back to her mother's side.

"I need an ambulance!" she screamed almost immediately.

On the other end of the line, the dispatcher responded, "I need an ambulance at…."

A loud groan called Bella's attention to her mother just

in time to see the woman's eyes roll back in her skull.

"Ma, please stay with me! The ambulance is on its way! Stay with me!" she screamed, groping her mother as hard as she could, attempting to nudge her back into consciousness.

She turned her attention to the cellphone, now covered in blood, and lifted it to her ear.

"I...I came in and found her stabbed." Bella tried as hard as she could not to stutter. "Someone attacked my mother!"

"Honey, what's your mother's name, and where are you?" the female dispatcher asked.

"Her name is Blossom Monroe," Bella replied as she snuck in occasional sniffs and shrieks of horror. "We are at 21 Parker's Street, right in the Blossom's Theater off the road!"

"And what's your name, honey?" the dispatcher inquired.

"My name is Bella...Bella Monroe," she managed to get out.

"Okay, Bella, I'm sending an ambulance right your way, darling. Keep applying pressure to your mother's wound until the ambulance gets there," the dispatcher advised.

Bella cast her phone aside while watching her mother begin to shudder. Suddenly, her limp body shot up in the air, and her fingers clawed at the floor.

"Mama," Bella muttered, knowing full well what was

going on.

Blossom was going into shock, and with nothing but her bloody hands, cracked voice, and misty eyes to attend to the woman, Bella felt useless. She placed her head atop her mother's chest and held onto her as tightly as she could, praying the faint heartbeat would grow louder.

"You'll be fine, Mama," she assured the cold-skinned woman before pulling her head away so she could look into her mother's eyes. "Remember all the plans we have? One of them is a week away, and you will be on your feet bubbly as ever and buoyant enough to be there."

Blossom Monroe wasn't a weakling in her heyday, and even while nearing sixty, she had not shown signs of growing frail. Yet, in that very moment, she could barely muster a smile or verbally reply to her daughter. It was telling enough to see her often-smiling lips stiffen and her eyes slowly losing their bright brown sparkle.

Bella Chloe Monroe lifted her mother off of the floor and cradled her in her arms while singing softly and sweetly into the woman's ear.

"I will never let you go," she muttered over and over again. "I don't know what went on here, but I don't care right now. All I want is for you to keep being strong until help arrives."

Lengthy cracks surfaced on Bella's heart. With her mother tightly lodged to her chest, her mind flustered with worrying thoughts of what might have happened to cause her mother to come back to an empty theater house alone. It wasn't unlike Blossom not to state what she intended to do, but that evening when they spoke, her mother had said nothing about meeting up with anyone.

Blossom coughed aloud, spitting blood onto Bella's arm and dress. In her weakened state, she managed to slowly lift her head and stare into her daughter's eyes.

"I'm still here, Mama," Bella assured the woman with a deceptive smile, fighting hard to hide her inner horrors.

Blossom finally managed a weak smile in return, but it wasn't fooling Bella.

"Who did this to you?" Bella asked her.

A teardrop rolled down Blossom's right cheek and stopped at the edge of her lip as she muttered, "I'm sorry."

The words came in a heaving tone and at a great cost just before Blossom coughed and retched up more blood, which landed on the ground and all over her daughter.

"You have nothing to be sorry about," Bella assured her mother while wiping away the teardrop from her face, then gently laced her mother's lips with a kiss. "All you have to do is keep being strong for me, for us, and for everything we have been through together."

Blossom cocked her head weakly and slowly began to clamp her eyelids shut.

14

"Ma! Ma! No! No! You need to stay with me!" Bella yelled, nudging her mother slightly and feeling the crack in her heart begin to lengthen and widen at the same time.

The flashing of blinding blue and red lights from outside the theater caught her attention and lit her face with a hopeful smile. Bella looked back down at her mother, and the tender breath of air she could still feel coursing out from her nostrils provided some sense of joy in her heart.

"Keep fighting, Ma," she whispered to her mother as two young men entered the theater and raced over to them.

"Is there anyone else in need of medical attention?" the first medic asked as he kneeled to tend to her mother, beginning to provide immediate medical treatment.

Bella shook her head aggressively and replied, "She's the only one. What took you so long?! What on earth took you so long!?"

She hurried to her feet and stood over the paramedic while he treated her mother and attempted to apply bandages over her wounds to help stabilize the bleeding.

"What's your relationship to her?" the second paramedic inquired. "We need to know her blood type, any medical conditions she may have, and other important information the doctors at the hospital might find useful while treating her."

"I'm her daughter," Bella answered in a sharp tone. "Anything you need to know, ask me. Ask me!"

"Oh my God, what happened?" a familiar voice asked, prompting Bella to project her vision towards the door.

"We need very few people in here at the moment, ma'am," the female paramedic told the woman.

Bella cut in immediately while nervously running her fingers through her hair. "She is family. She's my mother's sister."

Dalia hurried into the room just as the paramedic finished strapping Blossom atop a gurney.

"I was driving past and saw an ambulance outside," Dalia said with concern on her face. "What happened to my sister?"

Bella shook her head and shrugged her shoulders as she released a stream of tears. "I came to pick her up and found her in a pool of blood. She wouldn't say who did this to her."

Dalia cradled Bella's head to her chest and gently stroked her long hair while the paramedics sped off.

"We need to go with them," Bella said with urgency as she broke away from her aunt's embrace and raced to her car.

She briefly looked back to see her aunt still standing where her mother had been attacked, unwavering in her stance. Dalia showed little interest in going to the hospital.

The sight was puzzling, but Bella had no time to ponder on anything at that moment other than her wounded mother.

"You cannot go in there," one of the nurses told Bella, trying to keep her from entering the operating room for the umpteenth time.

"I just need to see her," Bella pleaded. "She will get better if I'm by her side. I know she wants me with her by her side."

A security guard walked over and stood in front of the double doors that led to the operating room, blocking Bella from running through them.

"We need you to remain calm and let the doctors do their job," the guard told her in a firm voice.

Keeping calm was the least of Bella's interest. Her best friend...her first love...her mother was fighting for her life, and Bella wanted to be with her for the battle.

Drowning her head between her hands, she closed her eyes as time slowly ticked away. Every couple of minutes, she would raise her head to glance at the doors the medical team had wheeled her mother through as they rushed her to the operating room. It had been three hours since they arrived at the hospital, and no update on her mother had been communicated to her.

Tired and aggrieved by the lack of response from the nurses, she marched towards the operating room but stopped dead in her tracks as the doors parted. Two men dressed in scrubs stood before her, their eyes leering at her.

"Are you Bella Monroe?" the man to her right asked while yanking off his face covering.

Bella nodded her head aggressively and shortened the distance between herself and the doctor.

"May I have a word with you over there?" the man asked.

Bella looked through the doors of the operating room and caught a glimpse of her mother's bed.

"Why isn't anyone with her? Why aren't they bringing her out?"

The questions pelted past her lips, and her knees began to grow weak.

"Please come with me," the doctor encouraged again.

Bella pulled herself together and made the brief walk into the empty waiting room where the doctor narrated at length, but all she heard were the last words a daughter wanted to hear about her mother.

With his outstretched hand resting lightly atop Bella's shoulder, the doctor told her, "I'm sorry," before exiting the room and disappearing from her sight.

Void consumed everything in Bella's sight; the doctors had failed her, and her mother had little time left. It felt like a poorly scripted movie, and all she could do was deny the reality as she turned around with weakened knees and a desperately reaching soul.

"Lies," she muttered in continuous denial as she made her way to her mother's ward.

I'm sorry, he had whispered. The words reverberated in Bella's head until she reached her mother's bedside.

Bella stood in silence, staring at her mother with nothing but questions and wishes. She fell to her knees and dug her elbows into the bed as she closed her eyes to pray. Her mother often said prayer is the key to all things, and while Bella wasn't as spiritually inclined as her mother, she did believe in God and His ability to come through in such hours of need.

The prayer was short, and words were scarce all through. Bella felt her throat constrict every time she wanted to find a new word; her larynx just wasn't up to the task. Parting her eyelids, she stared at her mother.

Blossom coughed softly, gently reached for the gas mask on her face, and yanked it aside.

"Bella," the woman called out weakly.

Bella snuck her fingers into her mother's and held onto them as tightly as possible.

"Don't…trust…her," Blossom whispered.

"You need to save your strength," Bella encouraged her mother. "You don't need to say a word."

Blossom tightened her grip around her daughter's fingers as hard as she could, tilted her head to the side, and with tears in her eyes, she whispered, "Dalia did this to me. Dalia did this…to…me."

Bella's eyes widened, her nostrils flared, and her hand began to tremble as she felt her mother's grip loosen.

"I love you." Blossom Monroe snuck the words out with her last heave, and her eyes rolled back as a long, steady blaring sound came from the EKG machine.

Bella stumbled backwards, stricken with shock and unable to speak. Her heart shattered into zillions of pieces, crashing down her chest and into her stomach as she watched the EKG machine flat-line. It was just as the doctor had said to her. Her mother only had a brief moment left before she would inevitably succumb to her injuries.

"I didn't get a chance to tell you that I love you, too," Bella whispered as warm, salty tears created tracks on her cheeks. "You cannot leave me yet!"

She reached for her mother's hand, held it tightly, and closed her eyes, wishing the world would come to an end at that very moment. The cold sting from her mother's hand sent shivers down her spine and set her heart ablaze. Blossom's blood shone brightly on her daughter's hand, causing a stir of discomforting reality as Bella took a step away from her mother.

A harrowing air of sadness engulfed the room, and darkness consumed Bella's consciousness within seconds. In a loud heap heard outside the hospital ward, Bella crashed to the ground, muttering incoherently while praying for the same fate as her mother's.

"Why?" Bella cried out in unbearable pain.

Chapter One

Shock and Disassociation

A weary smile lined her face while she doodled against an unseen canvas. The old grandfather clock chimed aloud for the fourth time that day, and like the other three times, it had alarmed the house of its existence. Bella remained still and focused on the drab wall before her. After all, it was the one thing that made sense since she gained consciousness.

"It's going to be the best one yet," she muttered to herself with a snicker. "The entire New York City awaits the event, Mother."

She took a long pause, sighed aloud, and resumed the doodling again, her eyes barely blinking and her lips continually murmuring incoherently.

"Bella," the same voice the lady had heard some minutes ago and the day before called out again. "Please talk to me. Say anything."

Bella gulped and felt a distaste mixed with disgust lining her throat. It was the exact feeling she felt after waking up to see they had washed her mother's blood off her hands. It was the same feeling she felt upon realizing they had attempted to erase her mother's essence and stench from her body.

"A-list Broadway actors and actresses should be there, Ma," she continued. "Kendall and I have a surprise for you."

Kendall shifted at the mention of her name and drew closer to Bella but stayed at arm's length, knowing better than to touch her. Her last attempt to do so had been met with fury and shrieks of uncontrollable cries.

"Dalia doesn't need to be there," Bella continued. "She is not welcomed, and I will personally see to it that she is kicked out," she added.

Bella sighed again, followed by a long pause and then a hearty chuckle before shaking her head.

"You know just what to say and when to say it, Ma." Bella giggled excitedly before turning her head to the left to stare at Kendall.

A discomforting wind howled against the windowpane, causing Kendall to shudder in fright before calming her nerves and drawing closer to Bella. Staring at Kendall with a blank expression, Bella tilted her head to the side and flashed a bland smile.

Kendall cleared her throat to speak. "I don't know what you're going through, but I wish I did so I can help you."

"What are you talking about?" Bella asked, her bland smile turning to a somewhat awkward one.

Kendall swallowed hard before continuing. "I'm talking about the fact that you have not spoken to me in days and won't leave this awfully stinking place. We are all worried about you."

With a shocked expression, Bella drew back and theatrically placed both hands on her chest to show she was at a loss about what her lover and partner was saying.

"I'm in my room, speaking with my mom, and all you've been is rude to me. I don't appreciate it," Bella retorted. "In fact, *we* don't appreciate it."

Kendall ran her fingers through Bella's hair, cast them down on her shoulders, and took in a few ample breaths while momentarily looking away from her.

"This isn't your room, Bella," Kendall muttered. "This is the attic where you moved most of your mom's things after her passing, and you haven't left this space in a week. You have not slept, eaten, or done anything but made me worry endlessly about you."

Bella's demeanor transformed within the blink of an eye, and worrisome frown lines emerged on her forehead.

"Murdered! She was murdered!" Bella screamed atop her guts. "It is rather convenient for you to claim she passed away, isn't it? How about we call it what it is? How about we talk about you, who, like everyone else, is playing a role in making sure I don't remember her!"

Kendall wore a confused expression on her face. "Why are you doing this to me? We are meant to be in this together, just like we have gone through everything together for the past six years!"

"And yet, you didn't believe me when I said Dalia was responsible!" Bella shot back. "You don't believe I am sane enough to remember my mom's dying words."

"That's not true. All I asked was for you to take some time to grieve while the police carried out their investigation," Kendall reiterated. "I love you, Bella, and I will do anything to help you get through this, but only if you let me."

Bella smirked in a mocking manner. "Then leave me alone."

Kendall got up from where she sat and headed for the door before stopping and turning around.

"Will you at least eat or drink something so you don't waste away in here?" she asked. "Blossom wouldn't have wanted you to starve yourself to death."

"Get out! Get the hell out!" Bella yelled, getting off her bed and storming toward Kendall. "How dare you! How dare you think you know what my mother wants!"

"I am sorry," Kendall replied, apologizing just before Bella shoved her out the door and slammed it shut in her face.

Dust fizzled through the air and invaded Bella's nostril, but she was too enraged to breathe or allow herself to choke on it. She marched back to her spot, sat down, and began doodling again as she had done before Kendall came into the room.

Warm tears rolled down her cheeks while she attempted to keep the same bland expression she had on for the past few hours. With the realization of how she had treated Kendall hitting her, the fact that her mother would have never approved of such actions, and the sad reality that she was all by herself in a desperately cold world, Bella couldn't keep it up anymore.

Finally, for the first time in a week since her mother's passing, she broke down and wailed profusely. Sprawled on the cold attic floor, covered in dust and dirt, she called out to Blossom at the top of her lungs, praying for a miracle and hoping the last seven days had been nothing but a terrible orchestrated joke.

"Why didn't you tell me what you were there for?"

she asked with intermittent sobs breaking through her voice. "I could have protected you. I could have been there for you."

It was the second most damning aspect to the realities hitting her while she cried.

"Today would have been your glory day! Today was meant to be the day New York City stood still at the mention of your name," Bella continued to lament while weeping.

The day, in particular, would have marked Blossom's show's premiere on Broadway. With a loud sniff, Bella sat up on the floor and stared into the darkness before her. In difference of what they had anticipated, the day brought nothing but sorrow, shear pain, and a reminder that her mother had been taken away at a time when her life had started to bloom.

Dalia. The name rang aloud in her head. Bella felt her nerves stiffen and her joints gain a rush of adrenalin.

She shot up from the floor and searched through large boxes containing her mother's belongings until she found the one she needed. Lying in the small box littered with belts and personal paraphernalia was a handgun her mother had never used and hardly ever took with her when she left the house. It was a gift from her father years ago before he left them.

"Dalia brought this on us," Bella grumbled, hoping

her mother could hear and approve of the thoughts coursing through her mind. "She took you away from me."

As Bella's newly found rage towards Dalia edged her towards the door, something else stopped her dead in her tracks—something her mother often said about family.

"Why would you even say that?" she grumbled to herself, then turned to look at the empty attic. "Family caused you this pain! Your unconditional love for family brought us this horror!"

She tossed the gun to the ground and stomped her feet hard, protesting her mother's constant clamoring about how family should always come first.

"She took you from me! She took you from ever getting to see your grandkids! Dalia took you from this world!" she screamed while scratching her fingers against the wooden door behind her until they began to bleed. Then she slumped to the floor in exhaustion.

Her fingers trembled while her consciousness weakened.

"This is a dream," she whispered. "This is a bad dream, and when I wake up, everything will be as it should."

The blood on her fingers brought a soothing yet damning feel to Bella. It reminded her of the last moments with her mother and the fact she had been alive then. It was all she wanted, and it was enough for her to find sleep for the first time in a week.

"Nobody can take you away from me, Mother," Bella reiterated with a sigh.

Hearing the creak of the door, she turned toward the sound and watched a dark figure enter the room.

Piercing pains at the basal region of her skull jolted Bella back into consciousness. The dark room she had fallen asleep in was no more, and the grandfather clock ticking away in the darkness couldn't be heard. It was easy to recognize where she was, and she hated it without a doubt.

"You're awake," Kendall spoke, catching her attention. "We were beginning to worry if you would pull through."

Bella stared down at the IV tube that ran from her left arm to a nutrient bag hanging on a metal pole beside the bed.

"What is this?" Bella inquired. "Where are my mother's things, and why did you take me away from my room?"

Kendall donned a confused expression on her face. "This is your room. This is our room and where we have spent the past few years."

Bella quickly turned her head to the side and looked at the bright wallpaper to her left.

"When do I get to go back to my room?" Bella asked without looking in Kendall's direction.

"You mean the attic," she replied, correcting Bella. "The same attic I walked into and saw you in shock and at possible risk of hypoglycemia."

Kendall got up from where she sat and walked around the bed so she could look at Bella.

"I get it," she whispered and reached out for Bella's hand. "You're hurting. I get it."

Bella sat up and snatched hard at Kendall's hand, forcing her on her knees, their faces close enough that she could taste her lover's labored breath.

"Did your only aunt murder your mother? Did you have to sit on the cold hard ground with your mother's dying body while you desperately prayed the worst wouldn't come?" she asked in a disturbing cynical tone.

Kendall pulled at her arm and tried to get away from Bella but to no avail.

"You're hurting me, Bella," Kendall pleaded. "All I've done is tried to help you."

Bella shook her head aggressively from side to side.

"No, all you've done is tried to make me forget my mother!"

In a burst of aggression, she shoved Kendall away before yanking out the IV and getting up to stand by her bed.

"I am sick and tired of you trying to teach me how to grieve when you cannot possibly imagine what I am going through!" Bella snapped. "If you really care to help, which I doubt you do, then stay the hell away from me!"

She turned away, ignoring Kendall's sobs, and began to drag her feet towards the door.

"Why should I trust you or anyone else when all I recall my mother ever doing was loving, trusting, and caring for others, only for her to get stabbed to death?" Bella asked right before exiting the room.

Kendall sniffed, wiped the tears from her eyes, and rose to her feet. "I am not your aunt, and the police are actively working on making sure whoever murdered your mother is brought to justice."

Bella turned around and let off a comical giggle. "*Whoever* murdered my mother? Didn't I already tell you who fucking murdered her?"

Kendall fell silent.

"You don't believe me, do you? Just like the cops don't believe me while they are still out there chasing their fucking tails," Bella snapped. "Yet you want me to trust you! You want me to believe this bullshit you're trying to shove down my throat is real!"

As far as Bella was concerned, the world was a cold place with no shelter.

"Then show me how to help you," Kendall pleaded. "Teach me how, and I swear to you on our love that I will stand by you every step of the way."

A buzzing sound from Bella's pants indicated she had received messages on her phone.

Bella waved her hands and shook her head. "What I need from you is to know that I want every single one of you off of my back."

She tucked her hand into her sweatpants, pulled out her cell phone, and held it up to see that she had thirty unread messages.

"Why should I do this? How will putting her so far away from my reach bring the peace and calm crudely taken from me?" Bella sobbed and spoke with a catch in her throat. "Who consoles me on the darkest days? Who casts away the worldly terrors when I find myself drowning?"

Kendall could provide no answers.

"Have I not lost enough? Must I watch her get sealed up without hopes of ever reaching her again?" Bella sobbed uncontrollably. "We will arrange the funeral service, but only when and how I want it," she added with a loud sigh. "My mother was a queen, and she deserves the best."

Kendall's face drowned with tears. Her eyes reddened and nostrils flared, but words never eased past her lips.

"I don't need anyone around me right now," Bella reiterated.

The person she wanted badly couldn't be reached, and regardless of how she tried to connect with her mother, everyone seemed interested in interrupting her moments. The thought of having to stand before her mother's casket and listen as people shared their fondest memories and expressed their condolences was too much for her.

"She deserves it, though," she reasoned with herself. "Ma deserves it."

Her heart broke at the thought of having to bury her mother, but the deed was done, and the funeral proceedings had to follow next.

"Please give me some time to think, and I will get back to you about when and how the arrangements should be made," Bella muttered. "On second thought, go ahead and make the arrangement, but I will have the final say."

She slammed the door behind her, then slowly crumbled to the ground and placed her head in between her knees as endless streams of tears mixed with guilt tore through her heart. This time around, the pain she felt in her chest was different; it wasn't just borne of pain but also guilt and betrayal.

"Forgive me, Kendall," she whispered to herself while

managing to crawl back to the attic.

It was the one place her mother's presence was ripe and filling. More so, she needed time alone to gather her composure for the funeral services.

"Help me, Ma," she cried after slamming the attic door shut behind her.

The emptiness in her world slowly dawned on her. Bella's confidant, protector, and ever-present mentor had been taken away from her, and she had to paddle through the turmoil alone. Even more damning to Bella was the fact that nobody seemed interested in taking her word for it that her aunt was responsible for her mother's death

"How can I make them believe me?!" Bella screamed in rage before slumping to her knees again.

Thoughts of how her aunt Dalia had cradled her head and consoled her that day at the theatre only made her cringe.

Chapter Two

Flowerless Funeral

Fourteen days, ten hours, and six minutes since her mother's death, Bella endured time as a daily nemesis and reminder of her troubles. Donning a long black dress that Kendall had bought for her, Bella watched as the flower bearer carried the spray of white roses past her. White roses were her mother's favorite. She knew her mother would have wanted them, which is why she made sure to purchase the beautiful spray. She considered it a final gesture of love for her mother.

Bella couldn't help but choke on a sob. Trailed by Kendall and the church pastor, Reverend Hopkins, she made her entrance with a raging heart and a sickened soul. The thought of her aunt Dalia still roaming free while the police continued their botched and baseless investigation stirred unpleasant thoughts through her head.

As if she could read her lover's mind, Kendall tapped Bella's shoulder tenderly and told her, "Today is for Blossom."

Bella sucked in ample air, held it tightly within her chest, and donned a frown behind the dark veil hanging from one of her mother's favorite Sunday school scarves.

Today is for Blossom. She felt Kendall's words of caution ring in her head again as the reverend urged her towards the church's doors.

Bella stood in the doorway, clenched her fists tightly, and choked hard on troubling bolus desperately forming as doubtful pellets in her throat. She spun around, cast off her scarf, and shook her head.

"I cannot do this! Oh my God, I cannot do this!"

Kendall reached out for her hand but was too late. Bella stormed off, racing as fast as her legs would carry her towards the church's vineyard.

"Bella!" Kendall called out while the reverend, who barely flinched, remained rooted in the spot where he stood.

Running until she was out of breath and almost crashing towards a large rock, Bella recovered her balance and settled herself on top of it. Heaving aloud, hyperventilating, and with copious amounts of tears racing down her cheeks, she growled aloud.

Kendall finally caught up to Bella. Panting, she stood with both hands on her hips while staring at Bella—both had bags beneath their eyes. Kendal, too, had suffered from the loss and was still suffering a great deal.

"If you cannot do this, I will stand by your decision," Kendall assured her. "Take a deep breath and relax. It will pass…eventually."

Bella looked up with baggy eyes and glassy vision.

"How can she be here after all she did?! Why is she here?!"

Kendall settled on top of a cylindrically cut rock to Bella's right and sighed. "I am equally as shocked as you, but don't let her steal your mother's moment."

"How do I go through the process of giving my mother the best eulogy or celebrating her life in the church she loved when her killer is seated right before me?" Bella asked. "Why do I have to go through such torment after everything I have already been through?"

Kendall stretched an arm around Bella and held her tightly to her chest before planting kisses on her forehead.

"You can pick a different seat and just ignore her presence until after the service."

Spotting Dalia seated in the region designated for family and friends created a distasteful stench to things for Bella.

"There are over two hundred and fifty people in there besides Dalia ready to celebrate your mother," Kendall reminded her. "One person should not matter to you right now. Blossom comes first, and she deserves this moment."

Without notice, Bella lifted her head from Kendall's warm and soothing embrace to stare into her lover's eyes.

"That one person is the reason we are here. Dalia is the reason my mother is lying in a casket right now and not with me, in person, alive!" Bella snapped. "Did you forget that?"

Falling silent, Kendall tucked her hands between her thighs and lowered her gaze.

Too rattled to sit and listen to Kendall try to be diplomatic about the chastening sight, Bella got up and began to pace around.

"Why will they not just arrest her? Why aren't they interested in locking that vile woman behind bars?" she asked without directing the questions to anyone in particular.

"I learned they called her in for questioning, and the investigation is underway," Kendall reiterated. "All we need is to trust the justice system to come through and put her behind bars."

Hearing Kendall note her belief that Dalia had done it

40

left Bella feeling a little relieved.

"People from all walks of life are here right now for Blossom, and these aren't just business associates." Kendall rose to her feet and approached Bella. "Some are college graduates she sponsored, church members she stood in the gap for and helped, and old-time friends she grew up with."

There were indeed notable people in the church when Bella took a sneak peek at those in attendance.

"Don't allow Dalia to make you desecrate your mother's final moments with her vitriol and betrayal," Kendall added.

Bella lifted her tear-filled face to the skies above and watched the clouds as they drifted by in the most beautiful and peaceful tone she had seen in a while. It brought back memories of childhood days when she and her mother would spend time cloud-watching right after church services. Being there brought a feeling of being watched over for Bella and strengthened her resolve to give her mother the best service.

"I think I can do it," she confessed positively to Kendall. "I want to do it for Ma."

Donning a bright smile on her face, Kendall wrapped her arms around Bella.

"They must be waiting for us," she whispered into Bella's ear, then took her by the hand and led her back to the church.

Bouts of mixed emotions coursed through Bella from the moment she walked into the church flanked with people who had come to celebrate her mother's life. She would have rather picked to have their presence at her mother's Broadway event the previous week, praising her mother and presenting her with all the accolades she rightly deserved.

The thought sent tears flooding uncontrollably down her face. However, the tears abruptly stopped when she walked past Dalia, who was dressed in a lengthy black dress that Blossom had purchased for her to wear during an event at their theatre a year before. Torn between ripping the dress off of Dalia's alabaster skin and kicking her out of the service, Bella remained as calm as she could. Being there with Kendall helped, providing moral backing through their long walk to the front of the church where the casket lay.

Looking stunning in a white silk dress, a diamond-encrusted tiara, and her favorite sapphire ring on her finger, Blossom displayed a smile on her face that both melted and heated Bella's heart. The slash wound on her neck was barely visible, and the funeral director had done an excellent job of hiding her other injuries.

"'Til we meet again, Mother," Bella muttered to the sweet-souled woman lying in rest before stepping aside so others could pay their last respects.

Loud cries erupted as friends and colleagues walked past Blossom's casket, including men in black suits who Kendall indicated to be with the New York Police Department. They shared their condolences with Bella briefly and moved on before Dalia came into sight.

"I will rip her head off if she touches that casket!" Bella growled in a low tone as she watched Dalia approach.

Kendall tucked her hand into Bella's and held it tightly before leaning sideways and whispering, "You cannot desecrate the church or your mother's service in any way."

Veins popped up on Bella's forehead as Dalia got closer. Stopping a few feet away from the casket, she turned her attention to Bella.

The lanky lady, who had a partly discolored incisor tooth, smiled before speaking to Bella.

"I know your mother and I didn't always get along, but in the end, she was family, and family always sticks together."

Bella felt her right foot shift in an angry reflex but not enough to defeat Kendall, who continued to hold her back from making a mess of the occasion.

"If there is anything at all that I can help you with, please don't hesitate to reach out to me," Dalia said with an extended arm.

The reverend looked from Dalia to Bella before fixating his gaze on Bella, who barely moved. Instead, she donned a smirk, turned away, and walked back to her seat with Kendall behind her. Her position on Dalia was clear as day, and she wasn't going to compromise her beliefs or grief at that particular moment.

"You did well, darling. You did well," Kendall said, praising Bella's ability to remain calm while they walked back to their seats.

Bella closed her eyes, leaned her head on the pew in front of her, and wept profusely.

"I want her dead...I want her dead."

There was no denying how terribly her heart felt. Her entire world now lay lifeless in a casket that would soon be buried six feet underground.

"How can anyone be so callous?" Bella asked as she continued to weep.

Her question went unanswered. Her wishes to have her mother back remained unanswered. The universe had turned its back on her.

The beautiful day extended towards the graveyard Bella had picked for her mother; the clouds hung above in bright blue and fluffy sight, while the sun shone brilliantly above the already dug grave. Bella wailed with emotions at the sight of her mother's final resting place, knowing Blossom had been ripped from her arms but not her heart.

Kendall remained by her side every step of the way as the pallbearers laid Blossom's beautiful casket into the dug ground, followed by the large bouquets from Bella and Kendall.

Reverend Hopkins cleared his throat and called everyone to order. "If there is anyone with the wish to send forth our beloved Blossom Monroe with items personal to their heart or to the family, would you kindly step forward?"

Confused, appalled, and in disbelief, Bella watched as only five people from a group of no less than a quarter of a million in attendance dropped off flowers at her mother's grave. The appalling sight undoubtedly showed just how little people regarded Blossom's passing even though they had chosen to attend. It diminished whatever level of interest Bella believed they had about her mother's demise.

"Is this all they could come through with?" Bella asked, looking to Reverend Hopkins. "Even the church couldn't muster more than one wilted rose for my mother's gravesite?"

Reverend Hopkins stuttered, struggling to muster the right words to the grieving and aggrieved Bella.

"This is just perfect!" Bella exclaimed sarcastically. "It makes everything perfect."

Loud murmuring erupted through the graveyard while large bodies paved the way for Dalia to walk through until she arrived feet away from Bella and a short distance from the casket that was about to be lowered into the ground.

"Over my dead body will you have anything to do here," Bella snapped, taking off her scarf and handing it to Kendall.

Dalia shrugged her shoulders, smirked wildly, and replied in a low tone, "I might be her adopted sister, but we are family. I have a right to be here just like her and even more."

Bella trailed Dalia's pointed finger towards Kendall and grew furious.

"I don't give a shit what you were to my mother. I know what you are, and in my book, you are a murderer." Bella let the words out without holding back.

Reverend Hopkins stepped in to quench the heated air, but Bella was in full emotional swing, and one man wasn't going to hold her back.

"I want her gone," she demanded. "I could tolerate

her shadiness, senile presence, and disgusting falsehood in the church, but not here."

Kendall turned her attention to Dalia. "You obviously aren't welcome here, and for peace to reign, I'd suggest you leave."

Frowning at Kendall, Dalia spat on the ground and shot back, "Don't you dare speak to me, you dirty abomination."

The words, without doubt, broke Bella's last bit of grace and sent her in full rage. She accosted Dalia and almost got close enough to claw her face when the detectives at the funeral service stepped in to stop the melee before it got out of hand.

"Why are you troubling me? I haven't done anything wrong," Dalia protested, trying her best to resist being cuffed.

"My name is Detective Larry, and for the past weeks, we have been filing a case against you as a suspect in the murder of Ms. Blossom Monroe," the detective informed Dalia. "Be advised that you are under arrest. Everything you say or do will be used against you in the court of law. You have a right to an attorney…"

Bella looked around for a cheer of some sort from those in attendance. Instead, they donned stoic expressions and looks of disbelief, which only further angered her about their notions and motives for even being at the burial service.

"First, they couldn't even come with flowers for my mother, and now, they desecrate the joy of having my mother's killer in custody with their looks of shock and confusion," Bella ranted before returning to the gravesite.

She understood her mother deserved more; Blossom had run herself into the ground for almost everyone in attendance, and their level of discord, disinterest, and obvious nonchalance left Bella feeling even more pained.

Reverend Hopkins demanded decorum from the ground and turned his attention to Bella.

"As the sole heir to Blossom, I'd like you to say a few words about your mother before we commence."

Delivering the eulogy was tough for Bella but standing before her mother's casket felt even harder—even more so considering the scanty floral representations of those in attendance. Her trust and hope in people waned as she took a moment to fight back her tears, focus her mind on the good times she shared with her mother, and prepare to share everything about her mother that she wanted people to remember.

After clearing her throat, Bella finally began to speak.

"Blossom Monroe was not just a mother. She was a friend, a nurturer, a human being of the highest and finest caliber…."

She took a long pause and struggled to get the words out as she took note of the faces in attendance. All she felt for every one of them was contempt for how little they valued her mother. She couldn't see past their inactions, and she definitely couldn't see past their treacherous perceptions when the cops led Dalia away.

It broke her heart and soured her trust in humanity.

For the second time, she cleared her throat and began her speech again.

"Blossom Monroe was not just a mother…"

Chapter Three

Psychological Torture

A thin smile graced Bella's face, and it felt as genuine as any she had summoned during her happiest moments. For the first time in days, the darkened clouds had steered clear of her emotions, and things felt a lot calmer than even she could have envisioned. It felt better for one reason and one alone—she was there, seated just a stool away from her and with the characteristic welcoming smile on her face.

"Who's up for more?" the sonorous voice echoed from across the marble kitchen table separating them.

Bella looked down at her half-empty plate, snatched up the last piece of blueberry pancake with her hand, and pushed the empty plate forward. The deliciously made pancakes aside, she wanted more of it and everything else in the room right there *and then. She wanted more of the sweet Saturday morning air emanating from the kitchen, more of the love-filled rhythm traveling across the entire house, and more of her mother.*

Blossom shot her daughter a wide smile, shook her head, and muttered, "Nice one, you little rascal."

It was a tease, and Bella welcomed it with a cheeky smile. She held up the half-eaten piece of pancake in her hand and stuffed it into her mouth as fast as she could; it was the rule after all, and she didn't have to wait for her mother to say it before she understood what would come next.

"You only get more after you've finished your meal," Blossom would note with a tender smile.

Bella held up both hands, showing her tiny grease-stained fingers, and replied in a characteristically cheeky manner, "I'm done, Ma."

Blossom tilted her head to the side, leaned on her left side, and scoffed. "You know, I used to call my mother Ma, too, and she often didn't like it until it grew on her."

Bella riddled her focus with the sight of her mother flipping the pancakes masterfully while she narrated one of her childhood tales. The stories made the moment sweeter, last longer, and above all, always brought a smile to her face when she heard her mother speak so fondly of her own mother, Bella's grandmother whom she never met.

"Someday, and I mean when you're grown, I can imagine your little girl calling you Ma and refusing to use the titles

Mom or Mother like most kids do," Blossom said, giggling before placing an extra plate of blueberry pancakes before Bella.

Bella smirked with excitement, gushing at the beautifully made plate and the ever-assuring gesture from her mother that they would always have each other's back. It was what such Saturdays brought to her—the reassurance of their perseverance and ability to weather any storm. It constantly reminded her who she had in her corner and who always projected a beautiful picture, for, at such times, things might not necessarily be as clear as day.

Stuffing her mouth as fast as she could, Bella halted and frowned. She caught her mother's eyes staring right back at her.

"What if I don't want to get married?" Bella asked. "Maybe I don't want to."

Blossom remained silent for a moment, took two steps back, and then leaned into the marble kitchen table.

"Why would you think such a thing, darling?"

Bella heaved aloud heavily and gently pushed her plate away before looking up at her mother.

"Because I want to be with you forever. I don't want anyone to take you away from me or come between us."

Blossom cackled wildly, shook her head, and shrugged her shoulders.

"Nobody can ever take me away from you, baby girl. It is always going to be you and me against the world, but you still need a family to stand by you when I am not around to do so."

Bella shook her head. "You are all I will ever need."

"That is just the teenager in you speaking, dear," Blossom assured her daughter. "Someday soon, you'll find true love, and we will live through the next chapter of your life together."

It sounded fair enough for Bella, who cocked her head before resuming her meal. Her mother's promises resonated through her as she scraped off the plate and placed it in the sink. Blossom never went back on her promises, and never at any point in time did she fail to be there for Bella as a father, mother, friend, best friend, and even a playmate.

"I always want to be with you, Ma," Bella told her mother one more time, prompting Blossom to run her fingers through the teenager's hair as she leaned over to plant a kiss on her forehead and then smile.

Poking a finger into Bella's chest, Blossom whispered, "As long as you have me in here, I will always be with you."

She stared into her mother's deep brown eyes, happily wallowing in them before the sound of their doorbell shattered her concentration and interrupted their little moment.

"I'll be back in a moment," Blossom told her daughter as she pulled away. "I love you and hope to see you soon."

The latter sentence came with an air of oddity to Bella as she stood by her mother's favorite kitchen stool, her eyes fixated on Blossom as she approached the door until her mother was out of her sight.

"What do you mean you hope to see me soon? I'm right

here, Ma!" She giggled innocently, shook her head, and turned around to wash the dishes.

A blood-curling screech tore through the house out of nowhere, and Bella recognized the voice. Her heart felt like it had stopped beating, and the entire scenery drowned out into an immense nightmare. Something had gone wrong...something had gone terribly wrong for her mother.

Bella raced out of the kitchen, heading for the front door, and felt her feet stuck regardless of how much she wanted to get ahead. Blossom was some feet away yet looked so far off in the distance. Judging by the stream of blood trickling and slowly pooling around her body, her mother was seriously hurt, but there was no helping whatever was holding Bella back.

"I'm coming, Ma!" Bella screamed. "I'm coming!"

The harder she tried, the farther Blossom and the door seemed to be from her. She was no use; she had failed her mother, and in it, she recognized an awful pain she had felt somewhere before.

"Ma!" Bella sat up from the cold floor where she had spent the past night staring out the window. She smelled of the stench of sweat as terror engulfed her.

Too afraid to part her eyes open, she knew what she was in that very moment—motherless, alone, and in the deep end of life that her evil aunt had plunged her into.

The previously bright room transformed into one of darkness, dirt, and foul stench. The sweet Saturday morning allure coming from the kitchen was no more, and musty air replaced her mother's wonderful cooking. She was far away from that place—the place where she learned about peace and love. She was no longer in the presence of the one soul who helped her attain sanity.

Bella was back in her harsh, troubling reality; she was back in the attic, struggling to make sense of what had become of her mother.

Slowly, the petrified lady looked down at her trembling fingers as a sea of sweat coursed down and invaded every surface area of her body. Her eyes widened in their sockets, threatening to fall out, and her lips muttered incoherently.

"I could have saved you," she muttered in a distinct tone. Images of the harrowing event at the theater flashed through her mind. "I could have stopped you from going there! I could have done something, anything, or just gone there myself!"

The shattered pieces of her heart began to melt with pain, and she growled hard, scratching against the floor and kicking at the dusty air.

"I could have done more to get to the door!" she expressed in disillusion about not saving her mother in her nightmare. "I could have done more to save you, Ma!"

Desperately trying to claw back the sweet scent from the pancakes, the kitchen, and every other moment she spent with her mother growing up, she found herself losing every time. Slowly and surely, they began to rot away, too, getting replaced by the harrowing reality that those moments she shared with her mother were long gone. The nightmare had only hurled through a fraction of her happy moment and then rammed a sledgehammer into it when she awakened to her reality.

Yet, Bella wanted those moments back—the ones where she spent most weekends trying out new recipes with Blossom; the ones that made her look forward to Sundays with Blossom so she could sneak and eat her mother's homemade cookies after church service; and those times when her mental support was available when she needed her.

"You could have taken me!" Bella looked to the drab-colored ceiling and tried to see through it as she spoke. "You could have saved her good soul and taken me!"

Her rage burst through the warm tears streaming down both sides of her face, the liquid threatening to burn through her skin like molten lava.

"She didn't deserve to die! She didn't deserve to miss seeing her grandkids!" she snapped angrily, screaming at the top of her lungs.

The clouds outside the house gathered and tucked the moon away as though they were terrified of what Bella's rage might do. She shot herself up from the floor and rammed her fist into the wall closest to her. The impact caused the old wood to budge and created a long scrap along the length of her hand.

"She did everything you ever asked of her!" she screamed while blood trickled down her arm. "God, why?!"

Memories from the thirty-eight beautiful years she spent with her mother flashed before her eyes—bittersweet moments she wanted to grab hold of and clutch tightly to her chest. The images faded from her mind, replaced with the events of the night when she found her mother. Bella shook her head aggressively, attempting to shrug it off, but it wasn't as easy as she was hoping it would be.

The harrowing events were there to stay, and there was no avoiding it. The blood, the blood-curling screams from her mother in her dream, and the heaving sounds Blossom made while lying on the ground of the theater room dying muddled up in Bella's head.

"Bella!"

The attic door swung open, and Kendall came running into the room. She wrapped her arms around Bella and cradled her head against her shoulder.

While stroking Bella's hair, Kendall whispered, "I'm here."

"Yeah, but my mother isn't," Bella shot back. "She is

not here to see us get married, or see us have kids as she always wanted, or watch us be awesome parents like she did with me."

Bella pulled herself away from Kendall and stared at her lover with dark, swollen eyes.

"Ma wouldn't even get married again or fall in love with another man because of me!" Bella screamed. "She gave me her time, her affection, and her love! She didn't want to share that with anyone else, and what did I do to repay her?"

Kendall stepped closer but stopped after taking only one step. "Don't see things that way, Bella. Please stop."

Bella smirked sarcastically. "Stop what, Kendall? Should I stop being sincere on how I failed Ma? How about the fact she wanted a grandchild, and I never thought of giving her one before she passed? How about the fact she accepted me, my sexual preference, and what I wanted above what every other person thinks, says, or projects?"

Kendall sighed, looked down at her feet, and then stood akimbo.

"Blossom was magnificent, and she remains one of the best people I have met in my life. But when you look at things from a better perspective, she will always be with you," Bella's lover tried to remind her. "Please don't damage your memories of her with self-guilt and hatred for the things you cannot control or change."

"But I could have done more!" Bella yelled. "I could have had more awesome trips to the beach, sweet-scented weekends, and love-filled trips with Ma if I had just put her first and not spent entire nights at some lame business meeting!"

An eerie silence intruded on their moment, and Kendal stepped forward with arms spread out before wrapping them around Bella.

"Your mother loved you so much, and I doubt she believes you are to blame for what someone else did," she whispered to Bella before planting a kiss on her neck. "I don't know how you feel or what you want to do to heal, but whatever the decision might be, I will be here."

Bella pulled away, and Kendall watched as her lover exited the room with the door left ajar.

"I know what I must do," Bella whispered to herself.

She would give anything to see her mother again, but first, there was a far more important aspect she had to take care of—dealing with the person responsible for her immeasurable loss.

"I know you don't approve of vengeance, Ma, but please forgive me." Bella felt her knees crumble as they met the hard floor.

Loud rumblings erupted from the heavens outside her window, followed by hundreds of marching raindrops atop her roof. The heavens wept with the motherless lady whose heart was set on nothing but trudging through the darkness before her.

"Wait on me, Ma," she whispered to herself, hoping her mother was listening. "I'll see you on the other side soon."

She could see everything before her: their weekend meetings, the trips they took together, and the learning moments she shared with her mother. She could project the peace and serene they often cheered for, just sitting right there in the distance if she could take the bold step and do what she desperately had to.

Pulling herself up, she dragged her sore feet and body to the stack of boxes against the wall and reached into the one on top. Carefully, she took out the silver Glock and smirked from ear to ear.

"Everything will be fine when it ends," she whispered to herself before gently placing the gun to her temple and closing her eyes.

Gently releasing the safety, she squeezed as hard as possible and heard the loud tick from the unloaded gun. The mentally torturing sound brought a renewed smile to her face. It was what she wanted, and she couldn't wait to have it. Well, after she made sure someone else had a taste of it—someone she desperately wanted to pay for the suffering she brought her mother and everyone else.

"Hold on, Ma," she whispered as another stream of hot tears rolled down her cheeks while the Glock remained pressed to her temple.

"I will not be motherless for long."

Chapter Four

Support? Yeah, right!

Bella took another long look out of the car, and for the umpteenth time, she wasn't sure she wanted to step out of it. It had been a week since the burial, and things had not gone on particularly as she would have expected. Asides from Kendall, nothing in her life bore a sense of normalcy or stability, for that matter. She was alone, motherless, and beginning to feel useless.

"Are you sure about this?" Kendall asked, looking out the window, as well.

Bella sighed. "I could have gotten here by myself."

The protest against allowing Kendall to drive her to her workplace was one she had lost. The woman was as stubborn as a honey badger and relentless in her desire to help fix things, as well. However, Bella wasn't sure she could be of much help. There was no getting a new mother, and she was definitely never going to see her mother again.

"I need to get things done through the proper channel and pick up some of the things I might need from my locker," she noted before shoving the car door open and stepping out.

Kendall did the same on her side of the car, slammed the door shut, and with a thin smile on her face, she smoothed down her hair.

"What are you doing?" Bella asked.

While maintaining the warm smile on her face, Kendall replied, "This is the first time you've stepped out of the house or even agreed to get something done, and I want to be of help any way I can."

Bella snickered in a demeaning tone and shook her head. "I don't need you here, Kendall! I never needed you to get me here in the first place. I just want to get in there, get my stuff, see one or two people, and get the hell out without being pitied and constantly moped at like a lost cause."

Kendall took a step away from the car, stared at Bella for a rather lengthy period, and then yanked the car door open to sit inside. Bella turned away and took two steps from the car. She heard the loud burst of cries from her lover but barely flinched as she marched ahead. Having Kendall there only made things feel worse. It brought the reality that she, too, could leave her as her mother just did.

Being motherless wasn't something she ever envisaged, and losing Kendall through unforeseen circumstances was another possibility she wanted to open her heart to. The naivety that came with life was no longer lost to her as she trudged towards the building before her.

"Just get your things and leave," she muttered to herself.

Her heart yearned to speak with one person, though— her best friend.

Bella shoved the doors open as hard as she could, stood stiff to the spot, and felt her eyes widen at the sight of bright colored balloons, sparkly lights hanging from the ceilings, and jubilant off-duty flight attendants jollying away. It was in stark contrast to the mood she had anticipated she would see. In fact, it was nothing close to how the air had been in the office space when one of them lost a beloved dog, talk less of a human being of such importance as her mother.

"Bella!" someone called out to her left.

Bella looked in the direction of where she was being called and caught sight of her boss holding a large chunk of cake in one hand and a coke in the other. Slowly, she swept her gaze through the entirety of the room, spotting nothing but shock, guilt, and a sense of oddity that she had appeared there in that very moment. It wasn't hard to know what it was; one of them was celebrating and in grand style, too.

"I didn't think you'd be coming back to the office so soon," Sheila Parker, the assistant manager, said as she raced over with the cake still in her hand.

Bella remained silent, waiting to hear the others speak, but nobody seemed interested or knowledgeable on communicating with her or even understood the need to approach someone who was motherless and grieving. Instead, they dug into their slices of cake, took sips from their drinks, and began easing out of the room.

One after the other, like a pack of humans avoiding a plague, they emptied the room, even taking with them the large cake she had seen on display upon first walking into the room.

"What do you need?" Sheila asked, still munching on her cake.

With a broken heart, a battered soul, and a flattened ego, Bella replied, "My…my locker."

Sheila nodded her head, patted her on the back, and whispered, "You can take your time. I will be with the girls in the conference room if you need anything else."

Sheila raced away, giggling to herself and consuming her consciousness with the cake, while Bella stood motionless and without understanding as to why she was suddenly an outcast in the same place she gave everything to. Memories of times she took days off to tend to some of her ill colleagues, the financial costs and implications she incurred while some of them struggled, and the times she stood in for them while they struggled with personal issues trudged through her mind like a waste.

"Why?" she asked without knowing who to speak to.

Turning her attention to the board to her right, she slowly approached the "Notice Board" to a harrowing sight that further sunk her stomach.

Off to the Bahamas on my vacation!!! XOXO... Melinda Tate, a note placed on a vacation spot on the notice board read.

Melinda Tate, her supposed best friend and longtime confidant who had not only missed the burial, but claimed she was ill and unable to attend, apparently just went on a vacation on the same day Bella's mother passed away.

Unsure of what to believe, unwilling to accept the reality before her, she tucked her hand into her purse and held two phones in her hand. One belonged to Kendall; she had picked it from the car without notice. Hurrying through her contact list, she dialed Melinda's cellphone and waited for it to connect. The phone rang but went to voicemail.

"What is going on?" she asked herself while loud cheers erupted from the conference room not far off from where she stood.

Too petrified to take more steps towards the locker room, she dialed Melinda's cellphone with Kendall's, praying and trying to convince herself that her best friend was probably sick as she had indicated weeks back, and not in the Bahamas as the notification card on the board read.

"Hello," Melinda's voice broke through.

Shaking violently, attempting not to stutter while she spoke, Bella replied, "Melinda, this is Bella."

The call came to an abrupt end with the blaring tone from the earpiece tearing through Bella's head. Her fist tightened around the cellphone, threatening to break it while her temple began to scorch with a terrible headache. There was no explaining why everyone seemed nonchalant about her ordeal; she would run herself into the ground for them

This cannot be right, she thought to herself as she proceeded to the locker room to get her laptop and other valuable items.

Stopped dead in her track right between the door leading into the locker room, Bella felt her eyes fill with tears. Her knees began to wobble, and her spine tingled with the most disturbing sensations yet.

"How could they?" she asked.

Unsure of how best to react, she turned around and headed back to the car where Kendall waited patiently for her.

She yanked the passenger door open, slid into the car, and leaned her head against the dashboard.

"Where are your things?" Kendall asked.

With tears in her eyes, Bella looked up and replied, "Take me to the church, please."

It was the one place she felt her mother's absence could and should be felt. Seeing how little they cared about her mother's demise at her workplace only made the feeling of being motherless unbearable.

"Okay," Kendall replied with a long sniff before rubbing the remaining tears from her eyes.

She had been crying, no doubt, but Bella could only sit in silence, feeling guilty about failing her mother and now Kendall. In the end, it was apparent the duo was the only ones who ever truly cared about her.

Bella turned to Kendall as she pulled the car out of the parking lot.

"Someone else has been allocated my locker."

Wearing a frown of discontent on her face, Kendall replied, "Is that legal? Why would they do something of such? What happens with your items in the locker?"

Bella sighed, looked out the window, and replied,

"Someone else needed it more than a motherless and obviously damaged lady. To think I paid for tickets for them to attend my mother's shows and often sent Christmas packages from my mother to them during the holidays."

Their lack of respect for the dead was glaring, but even more apparent was their little to no concern about helping Bella grieve. She realized all she had was herself and maybe the church.

No sooner had Kendall pulled into the church's parking space, Reverend Hopkins came running out of the church's doors. Almost falling over, the burly man managed to make it to the car. Out of breath, he intended on meeting with them before they got out of the car.

"Bella Monroe," the reverend said with a smile while avoiding eye contact with Kendall.

"Good afternoon, Reverend," Bella greeted politely. "Is there some place we can speak?"

Reverend Hopkins stole a glance towards the church doors, as did Bella, just in time to see two elderly women pulling the doors closed. Baffling, but not troubling enough to gain Bella's full attention, she turned back to look at the reverend, who was taking forever to answer.

"What do you want?" he finally asked in a stiff tone. "I have a meeting going on now, but I can answer any questions you might have right here."

Somewhat startled by his cold tone, Bella looked to Kendall and then to the reverend once again.

"I was hoping I could speak with you about everything going on, and maybe get consoling from the church as my mother and some of the elders proffered to grieving members."

The reverend sunk his head, took a moment to clear his throat, and then looked back up. "I'm sorry, but some of your mother's beliefs and stances do not allow you to qualify for counsel or any other business within this church."

Taken aback by the reverend's words, Bella shared a stoic look with Kendall before attempting to gain some clarity on the subject matter.

"My mother was the pioneer of almost every department in the parish, with hundreds of thousands of dollars, time and her sweat put into helping everyone in this same church," Bella reminded the obviously selectively-amnesic man.

He waved his hands and retorted, "Just being here, speaking with you and her, knowing full well what our stance against your life choices are, not only places me in a tight spot but jeopardizes my stern stance on illicit and immoral relationships in the church of Christ."

Kendall interjected. "In layman terms, you aren't allowing her into the church to get things belonging to her mother because we are lesbians?"

The reverend stuttered with his words before waving Kendall away.

"I will have your mother's items mailed to your house within the week, but you aren't welcomed here," he reiterated before turning around and marching back to the church doors.

Bella felt her head grow lighter. Her vision became hazy, and her belief system rattled to the core. Seeing how the church her mother served and gave her life to turned their backs on her within days of her demise was unrealistic and unbearable. It felt even more troubling because she understood the level of care shown to motherless individuals within the church. Blossom always found ways to stand for the motherless and did her best to provide for them and help them spiritually and emotionally until they could stand on their feet.

"This will not stand!" Bella refused to back down and get cheated of her spiritual rights as well as her mother's.

She stormed the church doors, shoved it open, and stood within its walls with bloodshot eyes while looking from the reverend to the elderlies.

"You have no right to be here!" Reverend Hopkins

alarmed. "Your kind has no right to be in here!"

"Yes," the elderlies within the church chorused in unison.

Kendall raced into the church, grabbed Bella by the arm, and attempted to get her out of there before things got out of hand.

Defiant about going away silently, Bella yelled, "What form of love do you preach?! What form of acceptance do you constantly preach when you condemn others at the expense of your hatred?!"

Seeing them smirk in her face and whispering incoherently about their disgust with her presence there with Kendall only infuriated her more.

"We don't need to be here," Kendall spoke in a firm tone while trying to guide Bella out.

Bella fell to her knees and wept bitterly as she leaned into the ground her mother once walked, danced and prayed through. She wished everything had been clearer before her mother passed; she wished Blossom could see the hypocrites she served and cared for. The once perfect floor, once sacred walls, and once favored building where she sought God, was no longer the same.

All it took was for her to become motherless, a troubling reality exposing those who claimed they practiced what God wanted.

"Blossom wasn't ever fully one of us," an elderly lady

named Esmeralda got up and said. "You can find another church that accepts your kind somewhere else."

Like a full quiver of arrows had been let loose into Bella's chest, the words smashed her hopes in people, the church, and in the jolly memories her mother built while serving the church.

"We should leave," Kendall pleaded with Bella.

Without further ado, Bella obliged, wiped herself clean, sighed exhaustively, and walked out of the church with hopes of never returning there.

The hellish day was a teaching moment the motherless woman would hold dear to her heart—one in which her mother's passing only seemed to lighten the mood at her office. Her best friend chose to be away in the Bahamas and ignore her calls, and the church she hoped would be the backbone she needed during her grieving and healing had cast her out as a sinner and an abomination on its grounds.

"Who would have thought I'd have nobody to see me through this harrowing period?" Bella snickered sarcastically as they returned to their car.

"You have me, Bella," Kendall assured her. "You will always have me."

Bella wished she could. Being motherless was proof she could lose anyone, and she wasn't going to allow herself to hold so much joy at heart anymore. It hurt her to see Kendall struggle to be there for her that much, but it hurt Bella even more knowing all good things come to an end.

Chapter Five

The Living-Absent Parent

The blue-rimmed moon lit the skies and shone brilliantly while it looked down on Bella. Such moments weren't ones she wanted to experience again. They brought harrowing thoughts of "what was," and the disturbing realities of "what could have been." Such moments were a stark reminder of what it was to be indeed motherless.

The stars had company, the moon had a support system in the alluring stars, and all Bella had was herself, an endless list of self-blame, memories of what she had, and unfulfilled promises of all she could have achieved with her mother. Stargazing was just another experience she wasn't ever going to have with her mother again, and it burned a bright hole into her heart.

Casting her gaze away from the hurting heavens, she stuck her hands into her coat's pockets, fixating her gaze on the restaurant across the road. Torn with emotions on what to do, how to go about her thoughts, and if it was even necessary to be there, she stood for a moment and took in the images.

He seemed so relaxed, unperturbed, and absolutely fine with not having her in his life any longer; at least, that was what his smiling face, cool demeanor, and nonchalance preached to her from afar. She wondered why her mother never mentioned him or gave room for Bella to learn anything about him while she was alive.

"Where is Daddy?" she remembered asking at one point in time when she was just ten.

Blossom, ever emotional and brave at the same time, had stroked Bella's head, brushed her fingers through her daughter's hair, and leaned over to plant a kiss on her forehead.

"I am and will always be your parent," she had replied. *"Why do you ask who your daddy is?"*

Bella had been teased in school by kids who claimed she didn't have a father, and the subject constantly ate at her young heart.

"Most kids at school have their fathers attend Father's Day with them," she had replied.

"How about I attend every single event with you henceforth?"

Blossom had asked. *"It does not matter what work I have to do; I will always be there."*

Blossom not only answered her daughter's queries brilliantly but made sure she fulfilled her promise until her last breath.

Recalling the memories forced her fists to ball tightly and her right hand to squeeze a photograph she had just found of her mother and the man smiling at customers in the restaurant before her. Both were dressed in white and smiled brilliantly for the camera. There were others of them sharing cakes and warm moments of hugs and tender kisses.

The revealing photographs only became clearer as Bella searched through the boxes one after the other. Notes, pictures, and more notes shared back and forth between her mother and the man she referred to as Michael Rhodes only confirmed one thing—they were a couple, and the man had hurt her mother in ways she couldn't quite understand.

"Is it wise to seek this man out?" Kendall had spoken against searching for the man Bella believed was her father. "I mean, your mother must have kept him away from you for a good reason."

Defiant to connect with some semblance of love from a parental figure, Bella shook her head and replied, "He is my father, and maybe he and Ma fell out or something, but I have to know, and he has to know the love of his life has passed away."

Even Kendall found those words tough to believe, and she shook her head fervently to make it known.

"I still don't think this is a good idea. I can be there for you, and I have shown how much I care about you through this entire ordeal," her partner noted. "I don't know what wound meeting this man will open, and I cannot stand to see you fall apart once again."

Bella's mind was made up, though. She had to meet with Michael and at least find out why he left his only daughter.

"What if he never knew about me?" she asked. "My mom never even mentioned him or told me anything about when he left or if he hurt her or if she hurt him."

"I guess Blossom did all of these for a good cause," Kendall reiterated.

Bella took another look at the dusty old photograph in her hand and felt her heart yearn for something; love, affection, or maybe just recognition from a living parent.

"I will find him, and I might need your help to navigate the rough terrains my mom enlisted as his last address," Bella said, looking up at Kendall.

A loud scoff escaped Kendall's lips, followed by the ever-willing lady shaking her head from side to side.

"We have been through a lot together already, and I

have seen you at your lowest. I have picked you up and listened to you insult me, take my help for granted and even claim I am a bother," Kendall reminded Bella in a hurt tone. "I will rather be all of those things than enable your journey through another path of potential hurt and heartbreak. I cannot handle it again."

"In other words, you aren't driving me to find him?" Bella asked to be clear on things.

Kendall shook her head. "I will not drive you towards heartbreak when you are so close to winning. Dalia is in jail, and she is bound to get sentenced any time soon! You finally manage your way out of the attic for the first time in four days, and all you want to do is go on this crazy hunt?"

"I need to know," Bella continued to sound defiant. "If there is a possibility that my father is out there looking for me, then I want to find him."

She desperately wanted to believe in those words even when she knew they were false. It was all a ruse to hide a deeper pain engulfing her with each passing day. The pain had grown beyond what she could handle inside the attic, and as she walked away from Kendall, she tucked the photograph in her pocket, took out her cellphone, and dialed Blossom's number once more.

For the umpteenth time in the past week, Blossom's phone rang aloud in the living room while Bella waited for her voice on the other end of the line.

"I found pictures of Michael, and I need to know if he knows I exist, Ma," she muttered into the phone after her call went to Blossom's voicemail. "I'll tell you whatever I find out about him when I get back."

She ended the call, tucked the phone back into her pocket, and proceeded towards preparing for her trip to find Michael.

Holding her cellphone to her ear one more time, Bella described Michael's appearance and all she had noticed about him over the past hour since she found him into her mother's voicemail. She ended the call, took in ample breath and steadied her nerve towards making the move across the street. It was the toughest decision she had made since her mother's burial, and one she couldn't help but feel might lead to more mental torture.

Racing across the street as fast as her legs could carry her, Bella walked into the coffee shop and headed straight for the service area where the clean-shaved man attended to the last customer in the store.

"We close in ten minutes, ma'am," he said to her, staring at her oddly.

Bella drowned herself with his image and perused

every surface of his face with her mind in hopes of never forgetting what he looked like. He was dashing to say the least and obviously stunning enough to get her mother's attention. His well-built frame was another alluring figure, not to mention the sweet southern accent with which he spoke.

"What do you care for?" he asked politely, wiping down the counter in a carefree attitude.

The stark resemblance was blinding for Bella and left her dumbfounded for a moment, but she yanked out the rumpled photograph in her pocket, laid it atop the counter, and dragged the man's attention to it. She had chosen the best one—one of Blossom and Michael kissing beneath a mistletoe.

"How did you get that?" Michael asked, looking up from the photograph.

"I should be asking why you left such a beautiful woman," Bella shot back in a feisty tone.

It wasn't how she had envisaged the reunion would go, but she was ready to beat answers out of the man without doubt.

"You left her, abandoned my mother, just like every other person has," Bella added. "I just want to know why."

Michael tossed the duster in his hand to the side, tucked his hands into his pockets, and replied, "Bella?"

Hearing Michael speak in her direction left a sour feeling in her throat. He knew her name and didn't seem too shocked about seeing her.

"How did you find me? Did Blossom set you up to this?" Michael asked, looking toward the door and then back to Bella. "I know we haven't spoken in some years, but I guess life caught up to the two of us."

He stopped for a brief moment and stared at her.

"You truly have her eyes, just as she always boasted," Michael continued. "Sorry I couldn't make it to her show. I didn't want things to become awkward between us like they were the last time we saw each other."

"What are you talking about?" Bella asked. "You and Ma haven't seen each other since you abandoned the both of us."

Michael rounded the counter and approached Bella.

"On the contrary, we did, but not on a really proper experience I must add."

He directed his gaze to the ground, looked back up, and held Bella in his glare.

"Why are you here?" he asked staunchly.

It wasn't the response a daughter would expect from her father, and nothing about the man's countenance indicated he was either excited or even emotional about seeing her.

"Did you love her?" Bella asked. "Why would any

father or husband leave either their daughter or wife without caring about what becomes of them?"

"This isn't something I want to get into, and I will advise you to leave my store immediately!" Michael's tone heightened.

Bella cackled irritatingly. "Did I strike a nerve? Are my words so brutally honest you aren't man enough to agree with me that you left my mother? All the while, you live out here serving doughnuts and coffee!"

She smacked a jar holding some loose change off of the counter and groveled in his face.

"I left because I found someone and because..." Michael yelled back at Bella and then mellowed towards the end, leaving his statement unfinished. "You really should leave."

Bella wasn't going anywhere until she found out if the man had any semblance of love for her or her mother. Being motherless made her feel vulnerable and lonely. She was without family as best as she was concerned, and the closest thing she had to a family was standing before her without any emotion whatsoever.

"You never loved her, did you?" Bella asked while she stared into the man's eyes.

He shook his head and answered truthfully. "I never did."

The piercing words rammed an immeasurable pain

through her chest.

"Even if I wanted to continue with the relationship, Blossom could never forgive me for having an affair while we were together," he added.

"You cheated on her? Who would have thought a man couldn't be loyal to his wife?" Bella sounded disgusted and sarcastic at the same time.

"I doubt you understand," he replied. "I doubt you'd be able to understand how much of a lie my relationship to your mother was until I finally found myself."

His words definitely left her confused.

"It was either I left and stayed true to the fact that I didn't love her or even cared about loving you, or my current relationship would have been a scandalous one for the church," he continued in a disheartened tone.

Bella took a breather, hoping to stay calm long enough to find out exactly what he was talking about.

"If you never loved Ma or me, why did you stay with her in the first place?" she asked in a hurtful tone.

Michael replied immediately without thinking. "Because the church wasn't going to accept it. I went into the marriage trying to hide who I am and to protect my partner."

Bella's eyes widened, and her clenched fists loosened.

"I'm gay, and your mother, my ex-wife, found out about my relationship with Hopkins," he explained.

Bella held up her hands, signaling him to stop

speaking. "You mean Reverend Hopkins?"

Michael cocked his head and smiled. "He wasn't a reverend back then, but it was either I stayed unhappy with your mother and kept lying to myself, or I pursued my happiness."

A sense of void engulfed Bella where she stood, and her ears began to ache at what she had just heard.

"Reverend Hopkins was your lover?" she asked to be clear about what he had just said.

"Well, he still is, and your mother always knew," he explained. "She never threatened to out me or him or even make a fuss about it to the church. It was easier to remain in touch with her kind heart because of that."

The irony at how she had been chastised and labeled an abomination by the church began to dawn on her. Her mother had endured, accepted and never castigated Reverend Hopkins for his sexuality, even though he wasn't being true to himself before the church.

"He should be here anytime now to get me home," Michael casually spoke before returning to the counter to clean up. "I am sorry about having no emotional attachment for you or your mother, but I have to do what makes me happy."

Bella understood the man, and while his inability to love her or even show any affection towards her cast a large veil of loneliness on the motherless lady once again,

her heart felt betrayed.

"All they did was stab Ma in the back even in her absence," she whispered to herself. "She accepted everyone for what they were, but all they did was cast memories of her down and try to tarnish the good life and legacy she lived."

Michael spun around as the last words escaped Bella's lips. "What do you mean lived?"

"Hello, honey," the familiar tone called out from the door, causing Bella and Michael to turn around.

Standing in the door was none other than Reverend Hopkins with blood draining from his face upon spotting Bella. A wild and rather vengeful smirk graced Bella's lips while she plotted the best way to get back at the ungrateful, spiteful and hypocritical reverend for all he had done to Blossom after her passing.

"Hello, Reverend Hopkins." Bella held a grin on her face.

Her cellphone buzzed hard within her pocket, prompting her to pull it out and read the message on the screen.

Dalia has been granted bail by the court. Reverend Hopkins and other members of the church footed her bail. Her sentencing is in a few months from now... Love, Kendall.

Motherless

The motherless lady let go of her phone and heard it drop onto the ground. Regrets fueled her in the very moment—ones of not having a mother, of not having a mother to protect her, and of not having her mother right there to witness the betrayal of this world.

Chapter Six

Determination Turned into Obsession

For the first time in weeks, the path had never felt clearer. Things slowly fell into place, but not entirely from a bright spot; the darkness continued to loom within Bella, and she could feel herself pulling away from everyone, including Kendall. It was easier finding strength in and with strangers than in those she had known and adored her whole life.

More so, there was something else she wasn't telling anyone; she was running and working against time. Every day since the burial and the events unfolding was a reminder of how many failures a lot of people from her mother's life had been, and Bella was bound to do everything she could to correct them. It didn't matter how, and it didn't matter through what means.

Barely three hours since her return from Japan and just a week since her travels to Africa, there was no stopping. All she could think about was the next plan she had to put into motion. Bella sat at the edge of her bed and counted the seconds as they ticked past fast. Her mind raced with thoughts about Kendall and how she might be fairing, but it wasn't the time to let her emotions run wild.

It was time to open a new chapter for her mother and not relent on all she had been able to accomplish within the past few months.

"Ms. Bella Monroe." Three subtle taps on her hotel room door alerted her of someone on the other side and caused her to straighten up a little.

"Come in," she ordered without looking towards the door.

The slim-built young man with eyeglasses that looked like thick goggles walked into the room and looked around briefly before settling his gaze on Bella.

"The mayor is on his way, and I'd like to know if you need anything else before the grand unveiling?" he asked.

Bella lifted her head and replied, "Just a moment alone for now. Thanks for asking, Thomas."

Thomas, the ever-polite travel companion and organizer of all her recent events, cocked his head, turned around, and headed for the door before halting just halfway through it.

"Aren't you going to take some rest?" he asked. "I know you did not hire me for my personal opinions, but I am worried you might burn out. That wouldn't be good for everything you have achieved so far."

Bella let off a soft cackle, shook her head, and replied, "We can always rest when we die, Thomas. I intend to do so only after I am dead."

He donned a frown for a minute and then slowly morphed the worrisome face into one big smile. It was evident the young man assumed his temporary boss was a joker or one who fancied making dark jokes, but she knew better and couldn't wait until everything was finally in place.

"See you in half an hour," Thomas spoke as he exited the room and pulled the door shut behind him.

Bella went to her knees, reached beneath her bed, and yanked out the glove box she had placed there as soon as she entered the room after checking in. Carefully, she removed the lid, stared at the box for a while, and smiled to herself. It was perfectly safe and lying in the state she had left it. She was worried someone might have taken it during her travels or her movements from one hotel to another.

She reached into the box, picked up the Glock, pressed it into her temple as she had done no less than six times within the past month, and gently squeezed. Hearing the gun tick with the trigger getting squeezed brought a lease of fresh breath through her lungs and got her heart pumping bitterly. It was a rush she never imagined she could want, and every time she held the gun, there was the deep desire to have it loaded, maybe without her knowledge, and maybe just once so it would hammer out something into her brain.

"It will be over soon, Ma." Bella giggled in a rather odd and excited manner. "I just need everything in place for you, and then she can have it."

It was a promise she was going to keep, even if it killed her doing so. Dalia was out and about, living her life, amassing supporters who claimed she had had not committed the crime, while others believed it was an act of self-defense after a heated argument had gone sour between two sisters.

Bella tucked the gun away, stood to her feet, and straightened her gown at its helms. She sucked in ample breath and felt some relaxing sting travel down her spine.

"In the next few weeks, nobody will dare forget about you, Ma," she promised Blossom. "Everything is in place, and it is one gorgeous step at a time."

She walked to an open briefcase seated just by the door, picked up the glossy magazine in view, and smirked wildly at the gorgeously spread image of her mother on one of New York's bestselling magazines. The magazine contained an article on the day her mother commissioned her theatre, and Blossom was in her favorite suit.

"You never aged," she said, praising her mother and hugging the magazine warmly before gently placing it back in the briefcase. She cleared her throat of the lumps of emotions slowly beginning to creep up. "There is room for one more."

She turned away, unlocked the door, and stepped out into the hallway. In majestic steps, Bella headed to the elevator, knowing she was about to commemorate her mother in ways many couldn't even dare or attempt to carry out. Blossom deserved the best, and she deserved to be remembered, and that was what her sole surviving heir planned to do until her dying breath.

Standing in the presence of Mayor Tom Holding, top stakeholders across New York, and none other than the president of one of the best publishing firms in the city, she felt like a queen amongst other royalties and wished her mother was there.

Stepping closer to Bella, Mayor Tom leaned in towards her and whispered into her left ear, "She would have loved this, wouldn't she?"

Bella held back a teardrop, smiled proudly, and whispered, "My mother would have screamed atop her guts to see herself right here and now and in such form."

Mayor Tom cocked his head, slid his hand into Bella's, and held it firmly.

"Thank you for constantly helping us remember how driven and dedicated Blossom was to the city and its people," he whispered. "It breaks my heart to lose a good friend in such a manner, and it hurt me even more after learning of your ordeal since you have been without a mother."

It didn't come easy. Bella could feel the scars she amassed through her ordeal in attempting to ensure her mother wasn't forgotten. Her theatre had been gathering dust since her demise, followed by notable workers absconding with her properties and those who claimed to care, not raising a finger to do anything about keeping her legacy.

"Those magazines enlisting her remarkable achievements were spot on, and don't even get me started on how you made the headlines as a motherless woman in search for justice," the mayor continued.

Bella scoffed, smiled, and continued to smile. She wasn't done yet, and she knew it. There was a lot still in store asides from having created a support group for those who have lost parental figures through a form of violence, those who sought comfort after losing a loved one, and those in general need of therapy towards finding some form of healing.

Her face and words were displayed on almost every flyer in New York City, and hardly a day went by without Bella Monroe telling Blossom Monroe's remarkable story of survival, grit, and love to someone.

"The moment has finally arrived," Mayor Tom said while he took permission from Bella to mount the stage.

An unveiled monument stood wrapped before the mayor while he gave his introductory speech to no less than five hundred people who had come to attend the event. Some had traveled across state lines to be there after hearing Bella's tales about her mother and how she had brutally lost her life.

"I'd like to call on Bella Monroe at this moment to do the honors of unveiling her mother, Blossom Monroe's statue at the heart of New York City." Mayor Tom held out his hand and pointed towards Bella. "Ladies and gentlemen, let's have a round of applause for Bella Monroe."

Bella stepped forward, took a spot by the mayor, and stared at the giant statue of her mother about to get commemorated. Emotions welled in her throat, her voice betrayed her, and her eyes finally released the copious amount of tears she had been fighting back. It was her first time crying since her meeting with her father, and it was the most fulfilling one she had ever had.

"I would love to dedicate this, the magazine features, the motherless babies' homes, the Blossom Monroe Foundation, and every other positive accomplishment hereon to my wonderful mother!" Her voice cracked, but she wasn't about to let that stop her.

Loud cheers of approval aired from supporters holding flags of Blossom Monroe and the Blossom Monroe Foundation in their hands.

"This for you, Ma." She looked to the heavens and smiled one last time before walking towards the statue to unveil it.

In that moment, Bella found some measure of joy amongst her hurt again.

Bella could feel herself getting familiar and comfortable with the current scenario. It was her third television appearance since her mother's statue unveiling, and she couldn't have been prouder to be there than she was on the previous shows.

She adjusted in her seat and readied herself to answer the interviewer's questions.

"I know I asked about the magazines you made about your mother's lifestyle and her deeds, the publishing company solely dedicated towards her remembrance, and the amazing works you've put into the Blossom Monroe Foundation, but how do you keep going and not feel drained?" the smartly dressed female presenter asked.

Bella wished she could answer as honestly as she could. Being motherless had driven her to the point of despair, self-loathing, and hatred in ways she could not particularly point out. Losing her mother had unearthed bouts of misery every time she came across people who had mothers. It left a sour taste on her tongue and a streak of envy in her path through the entire day.

"I cannot quit or get tired because if or when I do, then my mother's life here on earth might mean nothing," she smartly replied. "Blossom Monroe, my mother, lived an absolutely selfless life, and all I have done over the past months is to ensure every little girl out there knows they too can impact and impart loads of life in the world."

She took a long pause, leaned forward, and cast away some bouts of emotions slowly beginning to surface.

"I want her story told as it ought to, not diluted or defamed in any way," she added. "My mother deserved the best, and it is all I can offer her until my dying day."

An odd air of silence existed between the ladies before Bella managed a smile on her face.

"I am sure she is up there smiling down at your efforts and remarkable works not just for her, but in the lives of others who have been affected as you have," the interviewer noted. "I cannot even begin to imagine how much strength it takes to pick yourself up and say you want to have magazines done about your mother, run a publishing firm in her memory, and then have a statue of her on display in a notable arena in New York City."

The thoughts of her accomplishment thus far brought a sense of warmth to Bella, and she wouldn't have it any other way.

"I have a rather sensitive question for you, though."

The interviewer cleared her throat before crossing her legs.

"You can ask me anything," Bella replied cheerfully. "It is why I am here."

"How are you handling the fact that your aunt is being blamed for your mother's death? How do you feel about her being out on bail and that there are a select group of people who support her?" she asked.

It was a bitter question and one Bella would have preferred to avoid, but she wasn't about to back down from a fight. It wasn't in her to do so anymore.

"I have things in place to ensure someone or people like my aunt never get away with such harrowing acts on those who loved them, cared for them, and was willing to give them everything they needed," Bella replied without holding back. "I want to believe the law will take its hold on things, but my aunt is nothing but a disgusting lowlife who took advantage of my mother's trust and willingness to always entertain her cruel nature."

Bella fell silent momentarily, sighed aloud, and looked to the camera.

"Can you ever forgive her for making you motherless?" the interviewer asked. "We all know you titled your magazines *Motherless*, and most of what is in there depicts your aunt as a crazed woman who constantly betrayed your mother from the day she was adopted into your family."

Bella shook her head and replied, "Only God forgives, and I am human. I would forgive her if my mother were here right now. I would forgive her if she puts a bullet to her head and brings this pain I feel to a slow end."

It was as vivid and as candid as she could be.

"All I care about right now is honoring my mother's memory," Bella finally noted. "My aunt is of no consequence for now. She bears no importance for now."

Bella snuck her hand into her pocket and dug her nails into her thigh until she could feel herself hurt. She tried hard to hold a stern expression on her face while looking into the camera. She knew everything was about to end and really soon. Her revenge was on its way, and the plot was in the making for some time.

All she needed was a little more time to cement her mother's legacy before going after the vile creature that brought her life and world to its end. There was no chance in hell that she was going to let the woman who made her motherless walk away or even keep breathing life while Blossom was six feet under.

Consumed with hate, desire, and the overwhelming need to make things right, the motherless lady would avenge her mother's death...or die trying.

Chapter Seven

No Hitting Reset; You Live with the Pain

The bright lights slowly began to wane, and with each passing day, the interviews, magazines, and every other thing she had desperately tried to fill her life with had started to fade out as they should. Blossom Monroe's Foundation continued to bloom, though. However, Bella wilted on the inside, taking on a disturbing appearance that she noticed while gawking at her reflection in the shiny elevator doors.

Nervous, tired, drained, and without a doubt, nearing her wit's end, she clenched her fists, counted her breath, and waited for the door to chime open so she could gain some fresh air.

It should be easier from up there, she thought to herself.

The thought had hit her mind the night before while she stared out the attic window towards the road ahead. Feeling low on the inside, there was far too much holding her down, and she wondered how height might propel such disturbing feelings away. It was something she needed to try.

It was something she constantly felt every time the elevator ascended. It came with a soothing feeling—as though her problems were being cast off and left on the ground where they belonged. Taking elevator rides had slowly become an unhealthy obsession, too—a habit she perpetuated no less than sixteen times within a day just for the feel of it.

Like a junkie in need of their next fix, she leaped out of the elevator doors even before they fully parted, cast off her shoes, and raced towards the door leading to the rooftop. Her heart pounded hard in her chest, a sense of excitement fueled her soul, and her worries melted away, but not in entirety. She could still feel them, sense them, and without doubt, she knew they were there, waiting for her to come back to reality and start relieving them.

She would never have thought being motherless would mean her entire world would shatter in such a manner. She never could have seen herself spiraling down the rabid hole of insanity, even though she had done just about enough to ensure her mother's name, story, and legacy would live on. She had trust funds set up to ensure the foundation wasn't going to suffer or struggle, and the mayor had provided a relief fund of goodwill and in celebration of a theatre icon for her mother's foundation.

Bella wondered how and why she still couldn't find peace. Thoughts of what she needed to do continued to elude her. While her watch began to beep, indicating she had a meeting with her attorneys within the next half hour, she still couldn't contain any other thought in her mind other than the need to end it all and help herself restart in the afterlife.

"What more can I do, Ma?" she asked as the first breath of fresh air slapped her face as she stood on the rooftop of the law firm's building. "I don't know anymore."

She was lost, lonely, and desperate. Above all, she felt anxious about almost everything. She had not spoken with Kendall in three days and would rather not drag the poor lady through her mental torture even though she was already doing that to a good degree.

Taking a step at a time, growing in purpose and wondering what would become of her if she approached the edge of the building's roof, Bella stood within two feet of walking off the rooftop and sighed.

"What more can I do?" she asked in a tired voice while her head slumped downwards until her chin hammered into her chest. "How am I supposed to live life like this never happened!? Where do I draw strength?"

It felt surreal to see everyone living their best lives without a flicker of care that she was struggling. It was in stark difference to what her mother would have wanted. Blossom was known for putting her daughter first and above everything else, and Bella couldn't help but feel like she was at the back of the line where nobody wanted to reach.

While Kendall had done nothing but put her best foot forward in trying to ensure Bella didn't miss her mother, all she did was crave for the woman even more. The early morning toasts, the late-night movies, the lengthy talks until they ran out of call credits, and even the few times they haggled and argued felt like a lifetime ago.

Bella wanted it all back; she needed life to return to how it used to be.

"How do I live while you are alone on the other side?" she asked while she took two more steps forward and closed her eyes. "How do I navigate this dangerously lonely world without you?"

A harsh wind smashed into her face and brought with it the scent of rotten food, further highlighting how badly she needed to be away from the stinking world.

"Take me, Ma!" she pleaded. "I want no part of this! Help me leave this stinking world. I want to be with you."

Her cellphone buzzed wildly, breaking her focus and prompting her to peel her eyelids apart. Bella gently raised the phone to her ear and said nothing.

"Ms. Monroe," the husky-sounding man on the other end of the line said, "we have an appointment slated for nine, and I was wondering if you'd still be willing to make it."

Bella nodded and simply replied, "You should see me drop by soon."

She brought the call to an end, looked down below, and spotted she was a foot off of the building's rooftop already. Oddly, her heart felt calm and some measure of peace. She wanted to do it and hoped it would bring her everything she needed. She wondered what letting go would feel like. It was what her mother did when she passed away in the hospital and rendered her motherless; Blossom had let go and accepted fate as it had come.

At that moment, Bella looked up ahead. She spotted the New York Police Department's building in the distance, bringing the disturbing taste of betrayal she felt towards them for allowing Dalia's bail. The sight drew her right leg backwards, and she firmly rooted it atop the gravel ground on the building's rooftop. Freshly brewed adrenalin coursed through her veins while she contemplated what more she needed to do before finally surrendering her soul.

"Not yet," she heard herself whisper. "Not yet."

There was still more to do, and just before turning around, her peripheral vision grazed sight of Reverend Hopkins's church.

"Definitely not time to go yet," she said in renewed strength.

Three things had to be taken care of first. It would be a cold day in hell if she surrendered her life without getting them done.

"I am sorry, but I don't understand your reason, Ms. Monroe," the attorney said with a frown.

Bella shook her head, leaned back in her seat, and reiterated her desire. "There is nothing to understand here, Mr. Connor. I want to transfer all rights of ownership of estates, banking documents, and properties to my partner's name."

It was the second time she was making it clear while the man didn't seem particularly happy about hearing it.

"Are you being blackmailed, pressured, or coerced in any means or manner into making this happen?" he asked.

Bella shook her head. It was something she had come up with the night before after another groveling episode of hearing Kendall cry by herself while she remained locked in the attic tending to her mother's dust-laden boxes. It was high time she did something for the woman who had not only put her life on hold since Blossom died but hardly complained about Bella's cold, disconnected persona since she lost her mother.

"The plaintiff in mention will be your lover, Ms. Kendall Medina, correct?" the attorney asked again while scribbling on his notepad.

Bella sat up, adjusted her dress, and replied, "I am doing this because I have to, and it has nothing to do with being coerced. It might be the only chance I get to do this, and I need it handled before next week."

Mr. Connor cocked his head and sighed. "Is there a reason she isn't here with you?"

"I don't want her knowing any of this for now. You can reveal it to her in the right time and moment, but never before," she added. "This is my will and my wish."

"To be clear, you are making Kendall Medina the sole proprietor and holder of Power of Attorney over everything you own?" Mr. Connor asked one last time.

"Yes," Bella replied in a bold and distinct tone.

There was no turning back from there, and her attorney could very much tell as she stood to her feet and bade him goodbye with the purest and most disturbing smile she could muster.

Bella exited the room, walked into the elevator, and dialed Kendall's cellphone immediately.

"Hello," Kendall answered, picking up on the first ring. "I have been looking all over for you. I have been to the…"

"Pack up your bags, darling," Bella said, interrupting her in a buoyant tone. "I will be to you in half an hour, and we will be heading to Rome for a weekend getaway."

Kendall's excited breathing could be heard on the other end before a loud shriek of joy tore through the phone.

"I love you, Kendall," Bella whispered while watching the elevator doors shut.

Once again, the reality of what she had become, what she was, and all she could ever be was reflected to her from the elevator's shiny doors—a motherless lady desperately trying to navigate in a damaged world.

Bella took one more look at Kendall while she napped and envied the goodhearted woman. Kendall had everything going for her asides from being with a complicated, sorrowful, angry, and motherless woman. It was all Bella could think about, and with each thought came the overwhelming desire to remove herself and the source of

Kendall's suffering from the world.

With a sigh of relief, she turned her head to look out the window as she had done since she assumed her seat on the airplane. The clouds looked peaceful, calm, and ever so gentle—something that reminded her of how Blossom lived her life and yet brought Bella a stream of regret. Something about being up there in the office building hours ago had triggered a desire inside of her.

"I want to feel closer to you, Ma," she had said before buying the plane tickets. *"It is the only way I can stand the next few days."*

Being so close to the clouds and swimming in them brought a level of connection Bella wanted with her mother; she could feel the woman's warmth, embrace and presence hovering all around the plane. She could envision the wide smile on Blossom's face, the soft cackle that often lit up rooms, and the soulful eyes that constantly watched over her.

Right there on the plane, tucked in the clouds and far away from the blood-stained grounds on which her mother had been murdered, was where she wanted to be for the rest of her life. She wasn't going to have it any other way.

"Bella..." Kendall sat up and held a cheeky smile on her face while staring at Bella for a prolonged period.

Bella held her breath inward for a moment and then

parted her lips to speak. She had not spoken to Kendall since they boarded the plane, and while she hoped they could talk at length in Rome, she hoped things wouldn't get bitter there.

"I know the past few months haven't been the easiest on you, and I truly have a horrible deal to play in it," Bella began. "This trip cannot erase the stench of horrible behaviors I have shown you, but I am sorry. I am sorry I failed you, just as I am sorry I failed Ma."

Kendall continued to smile while she raised a finger to Bella's lips to stop her from speaking.

"I wasn't sure if you'd pull yourself together after all the energy and focus you put into ensuring Blossom lives in our hearts forever," she replied. "I wasn't sure I would have my babe back until you called and asked for this surprise trip. It is the one opportunity I have been badly craving for to be able to do this, and I want to believe we are back on track as we should."

Topping Kendall's list was her wish to visit Rome for a weekend with Bella, and it was the least Bella could do, knowing the days ahead were bound to be dark.

"I am sorry once again," Bella apologized with a tear forming in the corner of her left eye.

Kendall shook her head and retorted, "I'm sorry I never had the courage to do this. I am sorry I could never understand what it is to be motherless and all you struggled through after Blossom passed."

Carefully, she unbuckled herself from her seat, went down on a knee, and revealed a diamond-crusted ring she had hidden in her pocket.

Barely able to contain her emotions, Kendall smiled through tear-filled eyes and said, "Through the dark clouds and past the shimmering mornings, I always want to be by your side as your wife, Bella. Will you do me the honor of becoming mine forever?"

Lumps of anxiety formed in Bella's throat, and her chest pounded aggressively while she pondered on what response to give.

Amidst the clouds, Bella smiled and answered, "I do."

Screams of approval followed by raucous applause filled the air as Bella unbuckled herself so she could wrap her arms around Kendall and share a brief kiss with her lover.

"I would have it no other way," Bella added while looking into Kendall's soulful eyes.

They returned to their seats, fingers interlocked with each other's. Bella tilted her head towards the window so she could cry undisturbed. Her heart longed for Kendall, but it wanted to be in the clouds with her mother more than anything.

She knew what she must do; she knew what route she must take. Everything would come to its desired end, in due time, and soon enough.

Kendall tugged at Bella's hand, dragging her attention back to her partner.

"Don't ever leave me," Kendall stated, sounding more like a plea.

Bella consumed herself with the alluring sight outside her window and the feeling that she was high enough in the sky to feel her mother. The thought of the aircraft possibly crashing down to the earth, allowing Bella to see her mother even sooner, appealed to her. With the cynic thought circling her mind, she smiled and knew she would enjoy the flight.

Bella smiled, barely moving her lips to acknowledge or make the promise she wasn't ever going to do so. She could not lie before her mother, before the heavens, and before the same clouds that she desperately hoped to return.

Chapter Eight

Eye for an Eye, Bitch!

The weekend getaway in Rome drew to a close faster than Kendall had expected, but not as soon as Bella had planned it would. The tender moment in each other's arms and through the flights back paled in comparison to all Bella had going through her head. She wanted to be home, and upon walking through the door, she raced into the attic, locked the door behind her, and fell to her knees.

Drained, tired, and feeling weak from denying how badly she wanted to be by herself, with her mother, and dishing out punishments to those who deprived her of her happiness, it had eaten at her through the trip. It was even more difficult to accept the painful fact that Blossom would have loved a trip to Rome. She always fancied seeing a movie or a play in their historic theaters, and ending up there with Kendall was a trigger of emotions she could never have envisaged.

Kendall's footsteps hurried along the hallway and soon stopped in front of the attic door. "Is everything alright?"

Bella turned around, unlocked the door, and held the same misleading smile she had built across her face for the past two days.

"I am fine," she lied. "I just need to clean out some of Ma's stuff and get it over to the theater so the new staff can work on creating the memorial we talked about on our trip."

She searched Kendall's face for approval and show of belief, and it wasn't wanting as her partner took in all her lies—hook, line, and sinker.

"Do you need help getting them done?" Kendall asked.

Bella shook her head and smiled as best as she could. "You don't have to worry yourself. You have a work trip tomorrow, which means you cannot be late to the train station in a couple of hours."

Kendall's business trip was the icing on the cake that landed on Bella's thighs, and she couldn't feel any more blessed that things looked to be falling in place.

"I still have a couple of hours with you, and Rome

wasn't particularly long enough for us to connect totally," Kendall replied with a cheeky smile while she forced her way into the attic.

Bella cautiously leaned against the wall, pinning the Glock already in her hand to it with her back. Kendall leaned closer to her, wrapped her arms around Bella's neck, and planted tender kisses onto her face.

"I will always be with you," she promised Bella. "I don't care how rough things might get. I will always be yours."

Bella felt her teeth grind hard against one another while the gun slipped and landed on the ground in a loud thud. She stiffened as she watched Kendall take note of the awkward sound and then kneel towards the object to retrieve it.

Disappointment grew along Kendall's face as she held up the gun. "What is this?"

Bella felt her lips move and spill lies just as they had been doing for some time now.

"I was hoping on getting rid of it with all her stuff," she replied sternly and without stuttering.

It wasn't hard to see how difficult it was for Kendall to believe Bella's words as she tucked the gun into her pants and shook her head.

"I don't want you anywhere near this," she warned. "Please stay sane and safe for me."

An exhaustive sigh escaped Bella's lips, followed by a nod of acknowledgment. "Sure."

Kendall slid her lips between Bella's, kissing her passionately before exiting the attic and leaving the embattled lady with one big problem. Her weapon for revenge had been confiscated, and she had to find another means soon enough.

Hurriedly glancing at her watch and noting it was half-past two already, she kicked hard at the box of old clothes before her and cursed underneath her breath at what she perceived to be terrible luck.

"I cannot stop now," she convinced herself before exiting the attic. "I am too close to stop now."

It was the last place she had envisaged she would be in at that point in time.

Seated in silence, enjoying the darkness around her and in hopes it would consume her enough to get through her plans, Bella mumbled incoherently while picturing her mother's dire wounds over and over and again. The autopsy report revealed the wounds had been purposeful, deep, and laden with intent from whoever had struck her mother with the blade.

Whoever had done it had carried out the intent with

the desire to leave Bella motherless, or at least, that was how she saw it.

Forgive me, Ma, she thought to herself while she heard the sound of clicking heels in the hallway.

Soon enough, the door leading into the room creaked open. The large-framed figure walked in, followed by the clanking sound from the rusty light switch, which tore through the room before light burst through the previously dark space.

"Hello, Dalia," Bella whispered from where she sat.

Legs crossed on a wooden rocker, arms crossed over her chest, and eyes fixated on Dalia like a hawk would its prey, she smiled and watched the lady gasp in shock as though she had seen a ghost.

"What are you doing here?" Dalia asked, sounding entitled to the old shack she had been hiding off in for quite some time since she jumped bail. "What in God's awful world are you wearing around your neck?"

Bella looked to her chest, smiled, and replied, "Don't you recognize this? How can you not recognize this?"

"Why the fuck should I?!" Dalia yelled back, growing bold in her words as she attempted to charge towards Bella.

Unperturbed, without fear, and totally focused, Bella unveiled the silver caliber handgun she had previously tucked away in between her legs and watched Dalia's knees begin to wobble. Her once tensed-up nerves became flaccid, and her eyes widened in shock and showed how miserable she was about the outturn of events.

Retrieving the silencer she had tucked underneath her skirt, Bella screwed it onto the gun's nozzle and let off one accurate shot in Dalia's direction. The shot crumbled the lady to the ground in a loud, satisfying groan. She cursed, swore, and spat out in a horrified tone.

"What the fuck! What the fuck!?" Dalia screamed. "You bitch!"

Bella sighed, looked around the room once again, and smiled to herself.

"It wasn't particularly easy finding this hell hole of a place you've been hiding in like a rat, or even finding you for that matter," she explained to the groaning lady on the floor. "You see, I had to do a lot of unsavory things just to find you, and now that I'm here, seeing all you gave up with my mother and her affection just so you can live like a rat sickens me."

Slowly and majestically, she approached Dalia on the floor where she was still groaning and crying while lying in a puddle of blood.

Gently slapping Dalia's face to get her to remain conscious, Bella warned, "You shouldn't dare die on me yet. I still have a lot to ask you."

Niggling questions bit and tore through her heart from

the moment Blossom had mentioned Dalia as her attacker. It left Bella unable to comprehend what had transpired and why her mother had been murdered in the first place.

"I have nothing to tell you! You can shoot me all you bloody want, but I'm not telling you shit!" Dalia protested.

Bella cocked her head, pulled a rocking chair closer, and pressed her right leg hard into Dalia's open wound, causing the woman to shriek in agony.

"Every time I hear you scream, I feel blessed about this moment. I just want to hear it over and over again," she explained to Dalia. "In case you're wondering how I got this good with a gun, I've been practicing using bottles with your gruesome face plastered on them as targets."

It was something she did in secret, and she had grown to like it whenever Kendall went to work. It had become an enjoyable practice she itched badly to replicate on the real deal.

Dalia coughed aloud, rolled on her back, and looked to her shattered knee. "You are so going to jail for this! You are definitely fucking up now, even more than I am!"

Bella outstretched her arms to her sides and replied, "My life ended the day you murdered my mother and knowingly rendered me motherless. What more do I have to live for?"

The question ended with another gunshot into Dalia's

good knee, shattering the cap and exposing her bones with ease. The gruesome growl from the large-sized Puerto Rican lady filled the air in a melodious tune to Bella. She marveled in it, and like an opium addict, slowly began to feed off the high it gave her.

"Why did you do it, Dalia!?" she yelled into her evil aunt's face.

"She fucking deserved it!" Dalia shot back. "Your goody-two-shoes mother fucking deserved everything she got!"

Dalia's distasteful will was still intact, and it wasn't the reaction Bella had envisaged.

"I was just as good as those filthy theater actors!" Dalia screamed, groaning in between her words. "I deserved a shot up front and not behind the scenes!"

A thin frown invaded Bella's face while she looked down at her aunt.

"You stabbed your sister all because you weren't allowed to star in her show?" Bella asked in a confused tone. "She gave you a coveted spot even though we both know you are shit!"

She tossed her arms in the air in disbelief, erratically pacing the room and then stopping to look at her aunt before continuing to pace.

"Have you any idea what you took from me or what you took from the world!?" Bella asked her aunt with

122

tears now rolling down her face. "You ruined me! You shattered our worlds and then proceeded to hide like the coward you are in this God-forsaken place."

She kicked the rocking chair into the corner of the room, hearing it shatter before turning to look at Dalia once again.

"I slept in these clothes almost every night since you murdered my mother," Bella explained to her aunt, pointing to the ragged, bloodied skirt she donned. "It was the only way I could feel or sense my mother again. It was the only way I could hear her voice, feel her touch, or connect with her while the world moved on and forgot about her."

Dalia managed to crawl towards the door while Bella spoke. The big lady wasn't giving up that easy, and it only made Bella get angrier.

"I am not done recounting your sins to you, Aunt Dalia!" Bella screamed at her aunt before grabbing her by her dress and pulling her back into the room. "I don't believe you murdered Ma for a role in her show. I want to hear you say there was something more to it!"

Dalia spat out blood from between her teeth and held a terrified look in her eyes while Bella knelt over her and pinned her massive hands to the ground.

Gently pressing the nozzle of her gun into one of the open wounds on Dalia's legs, Bella asked again, "Was Ma ever bad to you?! Did she ever treat you like anything but a sister?!"

Dalia shook her head worryingly while she screamed for Bella to get off of her.

"Your mother was kind to me! She was kind and caring to me!" Dalia confessed with a copious amount of saliva racing down her lips. "I was enraged that she had everything going for her while I never could amount to anything no matter how hard I tried!"

Bella yanked the gun from the bleeding wound, stared into Dalia's face in silence, and felt a rush of sickening emotions begin to circle her soul. Her temple pounded with distaste, disdain, and absolute disrespect for what Dalia had subjected her family to.

"Was it all worth it?" she finally asked.

Dalia held tears in her eyes as she shook her head.

"Please forgive me," she begged. "Have mercy on me."

The words barely struck a note with Bella as she stared at the handgun lodged between her fingers. She had taken her time and put in so many resources for this very moment, bribing people to tell her where Dalia lived. Bella even acquired a spare key to her apartment.

"Do you have any idea why I have my mother's bloodied skirt on right now?' Bella asked.

The frightened-looking Dalia shook her head

aggressively.

"It was the last thing you saw her in before you took her life." Bella leaned closer into her aunt's chest and whispered, "And it's the last thing I want you to see me wear while I snuff the life out of you like you did my mother."

Dalia shrugged as hard as she could, throwing in her final burst of adrenalin in hopes of overpowering Bella. However, Bella's desire for vengeance and the mental tenacity built up over the past few months just for that moment wasn't going to ease off so easily.

"This shouldn't hurt for too long!" Bella cackled with the gun held high and jammed it right in Dalia's frightened, pale-looking face.

She watched her aunt's face twitch with genuine fear, and Bella flashed a satisfying look of Dalia being the prey. Without further ado, Bella squeezed the trigger hard, recalling her practice times and every single bottle with her aunt's face plastered on it as she felt the gun rip aloud and the bullet tore through Dalia's head.

In that split second, Bella saw her mother's lifeless face, felt her cries while she was being stabbed like an animal by her vicious aunt, and equally waited to hear Dalia's last breath just as she had heard her mother's in the hospital.

"I did it, Ma," Bella gushed with the most genuine

smile she could muster in months since the incident.

Slowly, she got on her feet, walked to the corner where the rocking chair had crashed earlier, and dug through the rubble of broken wood to acquire a tape recorder she had placed there earlier. She stopped the recorder, rewound it, and clicked play on it once again.

"I did it, Ma," the recording played aloud to Bella's satisfaction.

Dalia's recorded screams would be her soothing lullaby for the night, and her verification of avenging her mother's death would be the words she would wake up to the following morning. At least, for now, she would rest and finish up the one thing left in her grand plans.

It wasn't over for Bella Monroe. She still craved the clouds and her mother's endless warmth. There was one place she could get such undying warmth, presence, and affection. And she knew just how to get there.

She distanced herself from the church's rundown shack where Dalia had been hiding away. The realization that Reverend Hopkins and the church at large were willing to harbor a murderer just further stressed how hypocritical they were.

Chapter Nine

Evil Laid Bare

Counting her breath and praying to God for forgiveness, Bella relived those moments of joy and fellowship she had in the church with her mother. They were moments of pure bliss—periods of overwhelming fellowship in what they assumed was love and togetherness. They were moments of pure deceit coated with desire, falsehood, and envy.

Yet, those moments remained sacred because they were of ones she spent with Blossom.

Sunday mornings were often fun for Bella, and while she sat in her car, partly drenched in Dalia's blood, she could not help but smile. Parked in the exact spot her mother often chose because of its proximity to shade provided by a gorgeous looking tree to her right, memories of such days came flooding through.

Interestingly, she was dressed in a manner her mother would never have approved of for Sunday church service: dirty, untidy, torn, and bloodied attire.

Blossom Monroe had her rules, and always being clean at church was one she enforced strictly. There was no room for errors, no room for mishaps, and definitely no room for an untidy-looking daughter of hers walking through the church doors and making a terrible spectacle of herself before the church and God.

"Ma would be so furious," she teased herself and shook her head while she took a long breath, stared out her car window, and impatiently glanced at her watch once again.

The skies cleared ahead, bursting forth with golden rays as though darkness didn't loom within the church premise. Bella wondered how long it would take for anyone to notice Dalia was dead. She hoped they would, but not a moment too soon until she had gotten everything she needed in place.

"Here we go." She smiled to herself upon spotting the familiar brown-colored Volvo pull into the driveway.

It was the same one she had seen at Michael's place through the night while she carried out surveillance and the same car her mother had singlehandedly gifted the reverend for his birthday some years before. It brought a soft scoff from her lips. Seeing the hypocrite and liar ride in what her mother toiled to get with her hard-earned money only made her resolve towards him grow darker.

"One more, Ma." She looked to the dashboard of the rental car she was seated in and smiled.

Blossom's smiling face beamed right back at Bella from the photograph plastered into the dashboard. It was the same as the one they had put on display during her mother's burial proceedings, and even more, her favorite picture.

With another exhausting sigh, she shoved open the car door, slammed it shut, and hoped to gain the reverend's attention, but to no avail. The man, obviously still in a jolly mood about the wonderful night he shared with his lover, hummed his way towards the office just by the church's main entrance. She raced after him, biding her time until he stuck his keys into the office door before making her presence known.

"Pray for me, Reverend, for I have sinned," Bella whispered with a smirk on her face before pressing the nozzle of her gun into his back.

Reverend Hopkins stood upright, held his breath, and whispered, "What do you think you're doing?"

Bella replied, "Paying my mother's favorite reverend a visit and atoning for sins he constantly allows to slip under the rug in his church."

She shoved the gun harder into his back, causing a loud groan from the man while he hurriedly unlocked the door.

"Why are you in such a hurry, Reverend?" she asked. "Are you worried about someone walking in on us? Is there something you are hiding from your church or its members, Reverend Hopkins?"

Bella flicked the lights on and took a quick glance at her watch. It was some minutes past seven already and about fifteen minutes until Sunday school and the main service started.

Reverend Hopkins took off his coat, placed it atop his office desk, and turned to look at Bella. "What now?"

Bella shrugged her shoulders. "Nothing much really. Just a friendly visit in an attempt to ruin your life as you did mine and my mother's."

Sweeping her gaze around the room, she confirmed her presence alone with him before allowing herself to take a comfortable spot in one of the empty seats before him.

"How was your night with my father?" she asked.

Looking uncomfortable, Reverend Hopkins fumed, "This is not the place to speak of such matters!"

Bella shrugged her shoulders innocently. "What matters do you speak of? Do you mean being gay, or the fact that you rebuke homosexuality on the altar every blessed Sunday, and yet, practice the same thing you preach against behind closed doors?"

Blood rushed to the reverend's face just like when she spotted him at her father's coffee shop.

"Things aren't as easy as you want to make them seem," he noted. "I am the reverend of one of the biggest parishes in the entire New York, and that comes with some level of politics!"

His stance sent some embattled shivers down Bella's spine.

"You call desecrating God's preaching of love and acceptance as politics?" she asked. "You call turning your back on my mother's passing because she mothered a lesbian politics? You call conveniently sleeping with men and yet denying other young boys or men the opportunity to pursue their sexuality openly politics?"

Her contempt for him only grew with each word she aired past her lips.

"Your mother knew the rules! I wasn't in support of her openly boasting about you being a lesbian and being proud of it in the church!" he snapped back. "The reception you got after her demise was on her, not on me!"

"She was being a mother and a parent! She was taking responsibility for her daughter and fighting her battles in

131

ways adults like yourself and the liars hugging the altar cannot care to understand!" Bella retorted. "You do not shame her, but the God you serve and the lies you constantly live by!"

Reverend Hopkins charged towards Bella but stopped halfway upon realizing she was armed.

"I am not as harmless as my mother," she warned him. "I bite back and even harder than I am dealt. I fight for what I believe in and take vengeance against those who attempt to lead my life astray."

She got up from the seat and distanced herself from him while she walked over to the church's public address system's microphone in the corner of the room.

"I can almost perceive the lies from your mouth on this microphone, Reverend Hopkins," she teased. "I can smell the infidelity in your voice and the hypocrisy in your voice every time you sit here to address the church or play recordings of your biased preaching so they can live their lives off of your lies!"

"So what I sleep with men and hide it from the church," the reverend stated boastfully.

"I honestly don't care that you sleep with men," she reminded him. "I love everyone regardless of their sexuality, but you, my good man, have been calling people like us sinners in the public eye and in front of God."

His fists clenched and relaxed intermittently where he stood. Beads of sweat ran down the sides of his face while his lips curled and twitched in discomfort.

"My mother deserved better," she reminded him. "She deserved your support. She deserved your respect, and she definitely did not deserve having you hide away her killer on the same church premise she helped build and maintain."

A loud and irritating cackle filled the air while he made fun of her notions.

"Blossom was only a tool within the church, and her relevance died the moment she decided to act all mighty and better than me because she knew Michael and I were in a sexual relationship," he muttered in an angry tone.

"My mother never judged you or even cared about your relationship with my father!" Bella retorted. "Don't smear her personality and good heart with your lies!"

Almost without thought, he bit back. "But she paraded these grounds like she owned the place, expected to be worshipped and treated like a goddess who had no sin on her! I hated her guts from the very beginning and couldn't care less!"

The image became clearer, and Bella could see how terribly they had underestimated the church and those who led it.

"Blossom was an arrogant do-gooder, who didn't

belong amongst us!" he added.

"Yet, her financial girth was welcomed. Her constant donations, her sweat, blood, and dedication to the growth of the church and everyone in it was more than welcomed when she was alive!" Bella shot back. "Make that make sense to me, Reverend Hopkins."

An awkward silence dawned on them while the air in the room suddenly grew thinner.

"You never deserved my mother. She never deserved every hateful, homophobic, and distasteful member in this church," Bella spoke with a heavy heart.

Hot tears rolled down her cheeks and burnt her trembling lips. The realization that her mother had been a tool for the church hurt her beyond anything she could translate into words. It also sucked away the little joy she felt at killing Dalia or even confronting Reverend Hopkins.

"Well, you can take your leave now," the rude and arrogant reverend noted. "I have no idea what this little meeting of yours was meant to achieve, and unless you are willing to murder me with the gun in your hand, get the hell out of my fucking office!"

Bella held up the gun, stared at it for a moment, and answered, "You're right about killing you with this gun. I already murdered Dalia with it, so what should one more treacherous and despicable soul like yours mean to me?"

She watched him step backwards and struggle to grab his chair for cover, ultimately tumbling over.

"Just as I thought," Bella said, making jest of the man's feebleness. "All talk and little to no bite. My mother was every bit of the man you can never be and even more. I don't need to harm you today or right now."

She took a glance at her watch, took note of the time, and stepped aside for him to stare at the public address system behind her.

His lower jaw dropped, and his eyes threatened to pop out of their sockets. "You bitch! What have you done?!"

Bella shrugged, pointed to the switch on the public address system, and replied, "I came here without a plan actually and wasn't even sure if I was going to leave you alive by the time I exited that door."

She took a long pause, looked to the door and then back at him.

"Then I remembered how I listened to you sit in here and conveniently spill your hypocritical vitriol through this PA system and to those listening in the church," she explained. "In case you're too slow to realize what just happened, there are hundreds of Sunday school worshippers who just listened in on our little conversation in here."

With a grin on her face bound to cause anyone serious

nightmares, she watched the once confident and arrogant man become deflated. His entire being trembled as he rushed over to turn off the PA system still actively sharing their conversation with the church at large.

"You fucking bitch!" he exclaimed, groveling where he stood and attempting to race past her to tend to the nightmare from which he was desperately trying to get out.

Bella looked at the gun in her hand, shrugged her shoulders, and pointed it at the reverend.

"This isn't to kill you," she informed him. "I just wouldn't want you to make a run for it before you are able to get judged for your terrible actions."

With a perfect aim, she struck him hard in his right thigh and watched the short man crumble to the ground in a loud and painful groan.

"Goodbye, Reverend Hopkins."

She smiled at him as big as she could and exited the office.

Inconsolable and unable to cast away everything the reverend had said about her mother, Bella sat in the car and wept. A flood of tears rolling down her face barely prevented her from watching the church race to the office to tend to the reverend while nobody seemed interested in helping him.

His groveling for help while he bled out only landed on deaf ears while loud screams erupted all around the church as the minutes unfolded. Someone had found Dalia's dead body and alerted the entire church. Chaos erupted through the once peaceful setting, and the reality of their deeds slowly began to dawn on them.

Bella wished her mother was there to see the state of things for herself. She was glad, though; she had witnessed it all and would be able to narrate it to her dear mother when she finally met up with her. It was all she wanted, and what she looked forward to without a doubt.

A buzzing sound from her purse alerted her to Kendall's call, and Bella picked up with a clear voice.

"Hey, darling," Kendall called out. "What have you been up to?"

Bella put her car into reverse and backed out of the parking lot as she replied, "Just cleaning up some mess."

Feeling partly satisfied, she sped off before the cops could swarm the church.

Epilogue

Resting Peacefully

A swamp of dried leaves littered the grounds, reaching far and wide and bringing with it a rather nostalgic moment for Bella. She loved the snow, heavy piles of dead leaves, and every opportunity to play in them as a child. It wasn't to Blossom's liking, though. Having her nonchalant daughter dislodge the carefully raked stash of leaves back and all over her garden meant more work.

Carefully trudging her way through the stash of dead leaves, Bella finally stood before her mother's well-maintained and cleaned gravesite. White rose petals shone brilliantly atop the grave, with a smile greeting her face knowing she had paid for a lifetime of delivery to the gravesite for as long as her favorite florist shop still existed.

Going on a knee, she reached for one of the white roses and took a long sniff from it before asking, "Are you proud of me, Ma? Are you proud of all your daughter has achieved in your absence?"

Silence traveled across the graveyard, followed by chirping sounds from crickets as the day slowly wound to its end.

"I wasn't sure on how to go about it, but I guess you'll find a way to scold me when we meet again soon," she giggled. "Well, I'm a grown woman now, and you cannot handle me the same way you did when I was a kid, but you get the gist."

She laid down the rose and watched the moonlight reflect off of Blossom's picture just as a car's roaring sound came from downhill where the road was situated.

"I guess he has it already, Ma," she whispered to her mother once again before getting back on her feet. "I promise this isn't my last time visiting, Ma... I will be with you soon, or well, sooner than you can imagine."

She wanted to share so much with her mother: about her life since her mother's passing, about old times, and the possible future they could have led had her sister not decided to play God with Blossom's life. It was a reunion she desperately looked forward to, and for the past months that she had been visiting the grave daily, all she wanted was for her wish at reuniting with Blossom to come through.

"There is nothing else for me out here," she had told the woman repeatedly on every visit.

Well, there was one more thing out there for her to collect.

"This is a rather odd place and time to meet up with you, Ms. Bella," Attorney Tom said as he approached her in his oversized coat and somewhat worried-looking face.

Bella smiled, stretched out her hand, and replied, "Were you able to get it?"

He looked around once again, cocked his head, and answered, "You understand as a result of your recent issues with the church, they weren't entirely thrilled about selling to a Monroe."

"Which is why I needed you to buy it and resell," she reminded him. "Is it done now?"

"Sure," he replied. "All deeds and ownership of that particular grave spot by Ms. Blossom Monroe now belong to you."

The news brought a warm smile to Bella's face; it was all she needed and all that was left. She couldn't have ended what was an incredibly stressful day on a more positive note.

Attorney Tom reached into his coat and took out the large brown envelope before reluctantly handing it to her.

"Everything you need is in there, but I have a question if you don't mind indulging me."

"Go ahead," she encouraged him.

"Why the decision to buy a grave plot by your mother? Then you handed over all rights and Power of Attorney to your partner," he noted. "If I don't claim to be baffled, I will be lying."

Bella wished she could share her plans with him, but it would mean bringing in one more person to her harrowing realities or even granting someone knowledge to sabotage her opportunity to find the release and peace she dearly craved.

"Just thinking ahead, Tom," she put it simply. "When you experience as much as I have of human betrayal, it becomes necessary for you to cover your tracks."

She waved him away and headed for her rental car, hoping never to see the man ever again. Bella got in her car, wept for a minute, and ignited the engine before pulling away. Her heavy heart had begun to grow lighter, but she could sense fear slowly crawling in, and for what she hoped to achieve, there was no room for faltering emotions or thoughts.

Dressed in her favorite blue dress and gently lacing up the

buttons until they were all set, Bella looked around the room with a wide smile on her face. The image in itself and the setup were perfect, just as she had envisioned it to be for weeks.

"Perfect," she muttered.

She walked past the stacks of recently dusted boxes containing her mother's belongings, aligned every object seemingly out of place, and took a moment to enjoy the fact she had not been in her bedroom since her mother passed away. Life in the attic had been dangerously troubling, and clarity was harder to achieve in there.

As a result, it became evident she needed the purest environment to get her deeds done and wishes carried out.

"One more thing." She placed a finger to her lips while looking around the room. "There you are," she added with a wide smile and approached the bedside table.

Lying comfortably atop it was her favorite picture, one she took with Blossom on the day her mother pitched her first play to the public—the day her career got projected to stardom. It was one filled with untainted happiness, immeasurable positive memories, and above all, one of just Blossom and Bella.

Carefully pinning it to her breast pocket, she toggled the photograph until it was perfectly in place and then walked over to the foot of her bed, dragged the stool in the room directly beneath the ceiling fan, and climbed atop it. Reaching for the noose hanging from the ceiling, she recounted her blessings and final accomplishment one final time.

A teardrop leaked from the corner of her left eye while images of Kendall flashed before her mind. She had ensured Kendall would be financially taken care of and provided for the rest of her life. A smile trickled past her lips at how well Blossom Monroe Foundation was doing, alongside the publishing firm and other activities she had put in place to ensure her mother would be remembered.

Finally, she nestled thoughts of what it would feel like to lie beside her mother one last time. Her soul ached for her mother and being able to rest in peace by her for eternity.

In silence, and yet riddled with profound joy as the troubled soul she was, Bella reached for the noose, wrapped it around her neck, and kicked the stool away. It was all she wanted. It was all she had lived for since her mother passed. For Bella would rather die than live *motherless*.

They would meet again on the other side.

Suicide Prevention

The National Suicide Prevention Lifeline provides free and confidential support to people in suicidal crisis or emotional distress 24/7.

If you feel like harming yourself, reach out for help immediately.

Call: 1-800-273-8255

Website: https://suicidepreventionlifeline.org/

About The Author

Kinyatta E. Gray is a Best-Selling Author, Travel Influencer, and CEO of FlightsInStilettos, LLC.

Kinyatta's aspirations to become an author resulted from a heart-gripping moment in her mother's final moments of life. She committed to honoring her mother's legacy by becoming a published author. Kinyatta's mother wanted to be a published author but passed away in 2018 before realizing her dream.

Kinyatta has acquired the support of the biggest talent in the entertainment industry to support her books. The celebrities who have conveyed support for *30 Days*, the memoirs, are: TV personality Antoine Von Boozier; MaMa Kim from VH1 Love & Hip-Hop NYC; Florina

Kinyatta E. Gray

Kaja from Oxygen's *The Bad Girls Club*; CEO of New Jersey's largest radio station Time2 Grind; Always Ask Asia, Radio One Personality; and celebrity wardrobe stylist Jasmine Hill-Carter. Kinyatta's memoir was a sponsor of the Christmas event for Carol Maraj, the mother of hip-hop icon Nicki Minaj.

Rising in success, Kinyatta has been featured in a variety of press outlets: *iHeartRadio and Medium, Vine Magazine, Mogul, My Girl Gang, The Davi Magazine, Authority Magazine, Thrive Global, Pen Legacy, Daily Inside Scoop, Sheen Magazine, Fashion Bomb Daily, Billionaire Magazine, Los Angeles Blade, IMU Media, Definitely Amazing, Urban Magazine, Pretty Women Hustle Online, Afro.com, Bookstr, and, Yahoo.com* to name a few.

Websites: KinyattaGray.com, FlightsInStilettos.com, and Honoringmissbee.com

Podcast: Girls Love Flights, Feelings, and Fashion
https://kinyattagray.buzzsprout.com/

Magazine: FlightsInStilettos® Magazine
https://www.flightsinstilettos.com/purchase-print-magazine

Instagram: @kinyattagraytheauthor, @flightsinstilettos
Facebook: KinyattaGraytheauthor & MrsKinyatta

ALSO BY KINYATTA E. GRAY

BOOKS

30 Days: *Surviving the Trauma and Unexpected Loss of a Single Parent as an Only Child*

From Section 8 to C.E.O.

BOOK ANTHOLOGIES

Passing As Straight: *Beautiful Women Whose True Sexuality Went Undetected by a Judgmental Society*

I Survived: *True Stories of Domestic Violence Survivors and Their Courage to Live an Abuse-Free Life for Good (E-book)*

E-BOOK

So, You Want to Be an Author: *A Step-by-Step Guide for Aspiring Authors*

THE
KINYATTA E. GRAY
COLLECTION
AUTHOR • ADVOCATE • C.E.O. • INFLUENCER